The Renegade Lawyer

Legal Humor for Law Students,
Attorneys, and Other Interested
Third Parties

ERIC ZYLA

The Renegade Lawyer

Legal Humor for Law Students, Attorneys, and Other Interested Third Parties

Carson City, Nevada

First Edition / August 2007

Published by Xygnia, Inc.
www.Xygnia.com

www.RenegadeLawyer.com

Library of Congress Control Number: 2007934465

Publisher's Cataloging Information:
Zyla, Eric M.
   The renegade lawyer: legal humor for law students, attorneys, and other
   interested third parties / Eric Zyla
          xii, 272p.; 21cm.
   ISBN 978-1-934086-11-7   ISBN-10: 1-934086-11-8
   1. Wit & Humor—Law. 2. Law—Humor. I. Title

PN6231.L4Z9   ⌈Alternate catalogue   K184.Z9   ⌉
817.6—dc22   ⌊for law libraries   340.023—dc22 ⌋

Printed in the United States of America.
10 9 8 7 6 5 4 3 2

This book is dedicated to all the lawyers who read this book and get a good laugh out of it or find some common suffering that set lawyers apart from those outside the profession.

Acknowledgments

Thanks to my friends and colleagues who have shared their stories of legal woe with me and who have been able to laugh at the law and themselves. They are truly renegade lawyers.

Table of Contents

(Table of contents continued on next page)

Preface

My apologies for a serious preface to a humor book. As I discuss in the *Introduction* (because this *Preface* might go unread), no one wants a silly lawyer representing him or her in court. We want lawyers who will take our problems seriously. I am very serious when handling a client's case. In this book, however, I am inventing some humor to humanize the profession.

Many lawyers complain about their jobs but, frankly, the field of law is a good profession. While the hours might be long and the work stressful, it is usually intellectually challenging and ultimately rewarding. That reward can come in the form of a nice salary or simply from the satisfaction of helping clients. I like being a lawyer. I have been fortunate to work for and with very good lawyers who were also very good people.

Nevertheless, on occasion there are moments when being a lawyer is a frustrating experience. Of course, that is the same with any job. However, the law has taken on a glamour and mystique that many other professions fail to achieve. With such status comes the inevitable mockery. This book is not in any way meant to ridicule the profession but rather to lampoon it.

By poking fun at the various quirks in the profession, my

hope is that lawyers will be able to have a laugh at things they themselves have experienced. I further hope that nonlawyers and those people interested in becoming lawyers realize that we lawyers know what our profession is like and yet still choose to practice it.

This book is not an essay on the pros and cons of being a lawyer. And, while it is a humor book, it is not saying that we lawyers do not take our responsibilities quite seriously. Lawyers generally are not bad people, not hacks, and not devils. They are hard working people interested in solving dilemmas for their clients. But even hard working people need to laugh at themselves once in a while. So I ask that the lawyers who read this book understand and enjoy this send-up of the law. For nonlawyers reading this book, please have a good laugh and realize that lawyers are big enough to laugh at themselves.

Some legal humor consists of stories from the 1800s in England or of widows leaving their fortunes to their cats. Such humor does not convey the true state of the legal profession today. However, contemporary commentary on the legal profession can sometimes be nothing more than veiled contempt for the profession and people in it. Being a part of the profession, I want the world to know that lawyers are people, too. Everyone likes to complain about lawyers until they need one. Instead of complaints or derision, have a laugh instead.

Please enjoy this book and please remember not to take it seriously. Afterwards, we all seriously need to get back to work.

The Renegade Lawyer

*Legal Humor for Law Students,
Attorneys, and Other Interested
Third Parties*

INTRODUCTION

Can a Lawyer Smile?

The crime: I was seen smiling in the hallway of a law firm. I was a young associate lawyer. One of the partners asked me quite seriously, "I saw you smiling in the hall yesterday. What was that all about?"

Can a lawyer smile?
The short answer is no.
The long answer is the rest of this chapter.

I don't remember my exact reply to that partner but I do remember being exasperated at having to answer such a stupid question. Naturally, though, in order to keep my job, I had to appear nonplused, as if to say, certainly smiling is wrong, wrong, wrong.

But I didn't believe that smiling was wrong. I enjoyed my work. I was grateful that I was making a nice big lawyerly salary. I enjoyed being an attorney, specifically as a litigator of technology issues. I took depositions, went to court to argue motions, and did all the other tasks that a litigator normally does. However, I did them with a smile on my face in the office. I was smiling because I was happy and liked my job. That can be heresy in the legal profession.

Heresy!

You see, at the time I didn't realize that I was a renegade.

The practice of law has that certain *bah humbug* feel to it. Old Scrooge would feel so at home.

Years later I asked myself this question: "how can liking your job make you an outsider in the profession?" I'm not sure if there is an answer to that question. Was I Bob Crachet? Please note that we will not deal with Tiny Tim in this book.

Certainly, the law is a profession where image counts. You have to have the right demeanor as an attorney or else an opposing counsel might make a laughing stock out of you. You have to have a stern demeanor as a judge or else you will get poor ratings from the attorneys appearing before, you will face more appeals, and you just won't have that same credibility as the *hangin' judge* in the neighboring courtroom. You have to have the demeanor that inspires your clients that you will do the right job for them or else you won't get any clients and your existence as a lawyer will be short.

So many demeanors. So much fear to impart. And no three ghosts to come and correct the situation.

All these demeanors point to the particular stereotype we have implanted in our minds about lawyers and judges. Yes — we have implanted demeanors.

When Hollywood calls on Central Casting to deliver a judge or a lawyer, the happy smiley guy isn't the one they are picking. Sure they might pick William Shatner, but his character has a certain deviousness — it's not all humor.

I guess we could ponder all the reasons why that typical lawyer demeanor is so important. However, this is a humor book, so something funny would be more appropriate just about now. But seriously, it comes down to credibility, reliability, and a sense of stature. We want an imposing figure imposing justice. We want the *hangin' judge* not *judge friendly*.

Even if there is some logical or illogical argument that we want the *hangin' judge*, the tough attorney, the devious guy who will win us the case, does that demeanor have to take place inside the law firm, too?

The real concern is within the profession itself. Why can't a lawyer in the law firm be happy and chipper (chipper, not whistling, not dancing a *Singing in the Rain* song on the way to the firm's library, just chipper)?

Do the same games that we play in court or in front of clients need to be played in the confines of the office? You could argue that if some unsuspecting client arrives in the office and sees the lawyers smiling, then the whole profession will suffer. Goodness! What would he think? We would probably have to shoot him and that would be a loss of revenue. A bad situation all around.

Could you imagine walking into a law office where people were smiling and happy? It just would not seem like *the law* was being practiced there. Would it?

If you are too happy, people will wonder why. They will doubt your commitment, and they will question your seriousness, especially when practicing law.

On the other hand, perhaps lawyers are just unhappy people; so smiling is simply out of the question.

Many lawyers are unhappy in their chosen profession. They might not opt to commit suicide like the lawyer on the TV show *Scrubs*, but notice how on that show all the doctors are in the thick of life and lawyer is miserable. Better to be the janitor.

So, perhaps the miserable lawyers can't understand how anyone could be happy.

Is it a case of misery loves company or is it more dire? If someone is happy, does that happiness needs to be snuffed out at the earliest possible convenience?

Of course happiness is in the eyes of the beholder. While the typical legal practice does seem to avoid a lot tense sword battles fought in front of the local prince where a loss would mean that you have to marry to prince's ugly daughter (the one with the hump on her back), it still has a lot of distasteful jobs.

Before anyone says that working in a well-heated (or, depending on your climate, air-conditioned) office and writing a lot is not as distasteful as skinning the carcass off a dead shark in a cold, draughty *dead shark carcass place*, I should only say that *distasteful* is also in the eyes of the beholder.

You might have realized that lawyers are skinning carcasses off other sharks all the time. After the carcass skinning, or what we in the law refer to as the *trial*, is done, it is customary to go down to the pub (or a similarly situated drinking establishment) and have a few laughs. Yes, maybe lawyers aren't too dissimilar to *shark carcass skinners* after all.

Nonetheless, having that partner questioning my jovial attitude left me wondering if I was some kind of renegade to the legal profession. Was I a *renegade lawyer*?

What is a renegade lawyer?

Are you envisioning someone with a skull and crossed bones flag racing through a law office with a sword, a bad attitude, and shouting, "shiver me timbers"? That's not the image I was trying to convey.

However, I must admit that years ago, after having had surgery on my leg and an eye infection at the same time, I walked into my office with a crutch and an eye patch, whereupon a secretary noted that if I had a parrot on my shoulder then the picture would be complete.

Please remove that picture from your mind.

What I mean by *renegade lawyer* is not some sword-wielding maniac, but a lawyer who does not conform to the lawyers of our imaginations or Central Casting.

My advice is to read this book as it will hopefully put a smile on your face. If you're a lawyer already, smile with your office door closed. If you don't have an office, then you need a better job.

If you're not a lawyer and thinking of becoming one, then think about something else. Forestry management might be a good profession.

If you're not a lawyer and not thinking of becoming a lawyer, then you can smile a big smile. None of that schadenfreude stuff, though, please.[1]

Look before you leap or if you've already leapt then pray that you have a lifeline to pull yourself out of the quagmire that is the practice of law. The renegade's life isn't an easy one, but then my spirit hasn't been squashed yet. Yours hopefully won't be either.

Instead of moving on directly to chapter 1, please answer the silly questions on the next two pages and see if your answers match the correct silly answers, which follow thereafter.

Good luck.

Smile if you can.

---

[1] Schadenfreude: a German word meaning *getting pleasure out of another's suffering*. By the way, you might be alarmed that I have footnotes in a humor book. Please take note of the footnotes! As a lawyer, you will be inundated by them. In legal documents (and what isn't a legal document nowadays) footnotes sometimes have the most pertinent information. At other times, they are just repetitive garbage. In this book, even if they are either information or garbage, hopefully they are funny. Footnotes are themselves an example of schadenfreude from the document writer to the document reader. Enjoy them at your own risk.

Quiz concerning whether lawyers can smile

1. Sentence completion question. Concerning their jobs, lawyers are generally _____
    a. so miserable that they wish they had gone to medical school.
    b. so miserable that almost every day they hope for the Vikings (or some other barbarian group) to attack.
    c. so miserable that even Abbott & Costello, the Marx Brothers, Steve Martin, and Bill Murray combined can't make them smile.
    d. so miserable that most are on several different antidepressant drugs.
    e. not so miserable.

2. What would be the best title for the pie chart below?

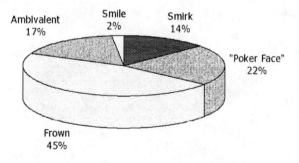

a. Facial expressions of lawyers after winning a case in court.

b. Facial expressions of lawyers after losing a case in court.

c. Facial expressions of lawyers after getting bonus at end of the year.

d. Facial expressions of lawyers after being served a piece of their favorite cake at their favorite restaurant.

e. All of the above.

3. Can a lawyer smile?

a. Yes, but only in the law library.

b. Yes, but only with the office door closed.

c. No, because in law school they beat out of you the emotion that would lead to smiling.

d. No, because they have no reason to smile.

e. Yes, but only when it's legally appropriate.

Quiz Answers

If you get all the answers correct you can smile. However, it must be a smirky smile of superiority and not a smile that you simply enjoyed yourself by taking a silly quiz. That type of smile is reserved to the people who answered most of the questions wrongly but having seen the correct answers, claim that they would have gotten the correct answer or answers had they known some special knowledge that would have allowed them to answer the questions correctly the first time around. The bonus smile is for anyone who smiled after that insufferably long and unexplanitive last sentence.

1. No lawyer would be so depressed as to go to medical school, so how could A be the answer? Certainly in every law class there is one person who went to medical school but we won't deal with that person here. B isn't the answer either because most lawyers realize that when the barbarians attack, few are left to sue them (the barbarians). The History Channel has more information about barbarians if you are interested. Answer C isn't correct either because studies prove that a lawyer can laugh if provoked by enough comedy, provided that the comedy is either top-notch or really silly (e.g. Three Stooges). Answer D isn't correct because most lawyers are on ulcer medication not antidepressants. Thus, answer E is the correct answer. Fooled? Most lawyers might

be miserable but not so miserable. Too fine of a distinction? Not really. You'll have a lot finer distinctions practicing law. Best get used to them now.

2. A very tricky question. Many of you will have chosen answer E "All of the above". Unfortunately, a title labeled "All the Above" doesn't make much sense. Have you ever seen a chart labeled "All the Above"? I didn't think so. The correct answer is C. Although studies show (secret studies that no one knows about) that 25% to 35% of attorneys are satisfied with their year-end bonuses, only 25% show it on their faces with a smile. The smirkers are usually trying not to smile and some of them are dissatisfied and have job offers elsewhere, so the joke is on the bonus giver. Answers A and B are not correct. Upon winning a trial, up to 4% of lawyers smile after hearing the news. After losing a trial, the number of lawyers smiling is also 4% and not 2%, except those 4% are contemplating suicide and are smiling only because they've gone bonkers. Answer D is not correct because lawyers expect to get their favorite piece of cake and eat it, too.

3. A lawyer can smile under certain circumstances, so C and D are wrong. While you probably think that they beat smiling out of you in law school, that is only partly true. Smiling in the law library can be

difficult to pull off. Actually I used to sit in the law library with my tie flung over my shoulder and was "kidded" each time by partners passing through the library asking if the room was windy. Funny? No, just obnoxious. Individuality must be stamped out at all costs (almost sounds like answer D could be a possibility). Anyway, A is wrong. B is also wrong, because you might have to share your office (beware 1st and 2nd year associates at major law firms) with a dork. Answer E is the right answer, although it is quite hard to think of an occasion.

Introduction Take-Aways

You might have thought the next chapter would follow, but first, we must review what we have learned from this chapter. Think of this past chapter as something much more than a mere introduction. Think of it as a chapter that might have actually had something relevant to the rest of the book. Even if you skipped this chapter, you still might be able to understand all you need to know by reading and absorbing (mentally absorbing, not like an amoeba absorbing) the take-away points below.

1. A lawyer can smile but not at work in the law firm, nor in court, nor any other place or situation that involves legal stuff.

2. A renegade lawyer might smile once in a while in violation of paragraph 1, above.

3. Choose to be a renegade once in a while.

4. Don't dress like a pirate.

5. Never have a quiz at the end of an introduction.

1

Why this Book is for You

This book may not be for you. Maybe you were thinking of buying it for yourself because you wanted something funny to read but then realized that you had no sense of humor. If you have no sense of humor, I advise you to replace the book on the shelf immediately. If you do have a sense of humor, then I hope *for your sake* that this book is funny.

Maybe this book is not for you because being a generous and kind person, you want to give it as a gift to someone else and you just could not think of a better gift. That doesn't mean that there aren't better gifts. It just means that you could not think of any. But let me reassure you that a gift is nice and you are thoughtful for giving it.

But wait, there's more! Besides being a book for yourself or a book for someone thinking about joining the legal profession, this book could be a good book for someone who just might like to hear funny things about the legal profession.

A humor book about the law. Doesn't get any funnier than the law, does it?

Okay, medicine, trash collection, dating, and dieting could all be funnier topics. Maybe even farm animal stories are funnier. But are they also funny and scary and possibly true all at the same time? That is something to ponder over.

Don't do that pondering now — wait until the end of the chapter.

Are you looking for a book that starts with the premise that the legal profession can be stuffy and insufferable? This book calls into question the idea that the legal profession, those defenders of your rights, is actually a good profession to be a part of.

I'm not saying it's a bad profession. I have been a lawyer for many years and even though it can be stressful, irritating, and daunting, the practice of law can also be interesting, absorbing, and fun. When I say fun, I mean fun. Writing a brief to the court and winning the motion can, in fact, be quite fun. But we won't be addressing that kind of fun here.

Are you looking for a book that deals with fishing? Oh, sorry, that's not this book. Perhaps I shouldn't have brought that up.

Are you looking for a book to talk a son, daughter,

spouse, loved one, friend, or enemy out of going to law school? Don't do that. They obviously have no choice but to go to law school and become a lawyer. What do you think they were going to do with that bachelor degree in political science? There are already too many political talk shows with commentators who know little or nothing about anything — and there's really nothing else to do with a political science degree.

People need to go to law school. How else will the legal profession become so overcrowded that the salaries will either come down to human levels or the economy is destroyed because of too much litigation? If the salaries of lawyers come down, then who in their right mind would want to become a lawyer? Yes, there will always be diehards, but then there are also people studying to be morticians so they can wind up on some hot new detective show on TV. As for the economy being destroyed, lawyers almost have that within their grasps now. Cue the evil laughter.

Using the law to get ahead

Lawyers like to make up a lot of stories. We call them *hypotheticals* because *hypothetical* is a five-syllable word and because it sounds so much more impressive than *made-up story*, which, you will note, has only four syllables. Also, you will note, that lawyers like to note a lot of things.

Our hypothetical involves two friends, Alice and Trixie. Alice wanted to go bang zoom to the moon and Trixie will do anything Alice does just to be part of the action. Both are married to really dumb guys, who are always trying to get ahead with *get rich quick* schemes. Alice has a better idea. She will go to law school and get rich by soaking the money out of what we lawyers like to call the *deep pockets*.

Deep pockets shouldn't in any way be confused with hot pockets, which are either delicious substitutes for actual meals or something associated with dancers.

Alice decides to apply to a law school (and Trixie does, too). They get into one of those really crappy schools that is only accredited by the Visigoths (or possibly their lesser known kin, the Ostrogoths). Upon graduating after 3 or 4 years, they each have well over $100,000 in debt, and so you might think that their *get rich quick* scheme failed. But wait, there's more!

Alice and Trixie wind up in a crappy law firm that pays far less than then all the hyped salaries. Better still, the firm isn't really the most honest place and after the partners rip off their clients, destroy the firm, and escape to the Bahamas, Alice and Trixie have to do temporary attorney work looking at countless documents and making even less money than at the dinky law firm with the added bonus of having no benefits, no job security, and no hope for advancement.

In the meantime, Alice's husband Ralph actually makes it big by selling vacuum cleaners door to door and Trixie's husband Ed wins the lottery. Bad news for Trixie, though, because just before he wins the lotto, Ed got his divorce from Trixie based on spousal abuse (Ed always seemed to have a bruise or bandage on his head but no one ever said anything). Ed had gone to a real law firm for legal advice but thankfully won the lottery to be able to pay for that legal advice. It appears to be a prerequisite today to need to win the lottery to pay for legal advice.

Alice on the other hand, killed Ralph before he could file for divorce.

So, there you have it: how to get rich becoming a lawyer. Sounds a little farfetched? You don't believe the amount of debt that each of our protagonists will have after graduating from law school? Maybe you don't believe that law school will take 3 or 4 years. I don't know what you don't believe, but believe it. There must be easier ways to becoming rich than by taking a college major that will lead nowhere. And I forgot to mention that Alice and Trixie get convicted of being unindicted co-conspirators (whatever that means) because of the old law firm's collapse.

Legal Reasoning

I've strayed a little off the path of why you would want to buy this book. I'm thinking it's because you are interested in the dieting advice in Chapter 8. And that doesn't mean to say that I think you need a diet. You look fine to me. Truly.

Perhaps you are just looking for an escape from the daily routine. Can't help you there.

I think the real reason why someone would want this book is because I don't care about the rules. Take grammar for instance. You might also like to use bad grammar. Then this book is especially for you because I'm not going to conform to anyone's rules and all my grammatical mistakes are actually done on purpose.

This book does not have stories about the hilarious practice of law in the 1800s or in England. It does not have funny stories about how a cow inherited a million dollars, how someone sued for something stupid, or any stuff like that. If you are craving stories like those, they're not here. Maybe I can make up stuff like that for a second book.

This book *primarily* contains little cute stories about the contemporary practice of law based on actual events or stuff actually made up. *Secondarily*, this book contains fun and exciting little quizzes that you can take to see if your knowledge of the legal profession actually comports with reality. *Tertiarily*, this book avoids all that *party of the first part* crap, except where it's really needed. And *quartinarily* (I don't even know if there is such a word, but I am sure that if it does exist, it exists in the law and especially in legal documents like many of the contracts you have lying about your house — perhaps it's part of your credit card agreement or maybe it's in your mortgage application), this book has other stuff (I lost track of what I was going to say after writing that longwinded parenthetical about *quartinarily*).

This is a book for people thinking:

- *Hey, before I become a lawyer, perhaps I will read a book that supposedly takes a humorous but honest look at the legal profession.*
- *Hey, this book has a neat cover and it deals with the law, let's get it.*
- *Hey, it's a day of the week with 'day' in it, so I*

*should buy a book and this one looks good enough
to read.*

This book is also for people who are thinking other thoughts
or not thinking at all (that's my take on inclusiveness).

After having said all that nonsense, this book is a book
about the law, so it certainly must drone on a bit longer than,
say, a book on how to cook squirrels found in your
neighbor's yard. Just a little legal advice: if you are cooking
such captured squirrels, then don't ask you neighbor if he's
got milk.

I realize that reading the *Introduction* was wasting your
time, so that's why I gave this one a number and a title. No
matter whether you bought this book for yourself or
someone you moderately like, you've got to stop reading this
chapter get on to chapters that have higher numbers atop
them and hopefully more substance within.

For instance, if you immediately turned to page 117 and
started reading at the last sentence of the second to last
paragraph, you would have a brief taste at how thoroughly
many lawyers read things. Start in the middle, read
haphazardly, and then argue. Unfortunately, this book is
meant to be read from the beginning (even including the
Preface).

Before you turn to chapter 8 (which would actually be a
funnier chapter to start with) and begin reading something in
the middle, you should take the quiz that follows and see if
you really have the mindset to read a book about law.

Answers follow the quiz.

Don't cheat.

Quiz to see that this book is really for you

1. A small shopkeeper slips and falls in his own store. Whom should he sue?
   a. The shop around the corner (because that damn Meg Ryan can be so annoying).
   b. Whom? What's with the fancy objective case pronoun usage?
   c. Himself, obviously. He will get to enjoy the insurance money.
   d. The chemical company who made the cleaning fluid; the idiot who cleaned the floor; and the big oil companies.
   e. All of the above.

2. Complete the following sentence: One in the hand is worth two in the _____.
   a. Don't answer this question out loud.
   b. "insurance fraud racket"
   c. "the grassy knoll"
   d. "hands"
   e. "judge's hand"

3. Fallible human beings make laws and thus the law is fallible. I refer here specifically to traffic laws. I once got a ticket for speeding and had to pay a huge fine. Then two weeks later they raised the speed limit there above the speed I had been going. Two weeks after that, I got a computer generated letter

from the state of California to be a more careful driver.

    a.   That's not a question.

    b.   You are outraged!

    c.   You aren't outraged.

    d.   So let me get this straight. You were driving 65 in a 55 zone and got a ticket and then a couple of weeks later they raised the speed limit to 70 and a few weeks after that you got a letter from the state telling you to drive better. And you paid the fine. I'm just trying to understand this. So, you were breaking the law when you got the ticket but you're complaining that there's some injustice in the fact that shortly thereafter they raised the speed limit but still reprimanded you. Is this some kind of complaint or commentary on the law or that the law and justice are two separate things? What's the point that you are trying to make?

    e.   Judge's hand.

4.   Reading Comprehension (yes, I know you hate the reading comprehension question but it's something that lawyers do every day - - I mean trying to comprehend things). Alice got rich by going to law school because

    a.   She knew how to murder Ralph and get away with it because of her new found knowledge from law school.

b. She knew how to murder Ralph and get away with it because she watched a lot of TV shows and always wanted to be a mortician.

c. She killed Ralph and got his money and the reading selection was silent as to how she got away with it but we must assume that Trixie was involved and that Trixie won't take the fall and watch Alice get off scott free.

d. She married Ed.

e. Judge's hand.

5. You need this book to help someone make a decision about whether to go to law school or to become a lawyer because

a. You love them and want to protect them from the hardship of attending law school, taking the bar exam, and working as an attorney.

b. You hate them and want to make sure they never make the kind of money that you hear that lawyers make.

c. You love them and want them to make the kind of money that you hear lawyers make and be able to smile while making that money.

d. You hate them and you want them to get the

idea that practicing law can be a fun time.

e.   Judge's hand.

Quiz answers

Give yourself 100 points for each right answer, 50 points for each wrong answer, 100 points for each really wrong answer, and reflect on the nature of life.

1. The answer is E. Yes, E! Don't whine that B isn't really an answer so how can E, which contains B, be the right answer, it just is. Let's go through each of the other responses to see where you made your big mistake. Answer C would seem to make the most sense because you always want to get the insurance money. But, then there's answer D. You always want to sue the companies that made the stuff, someone who was associated with the stuff, and the big oil companies. You can't leave the big oil companies out of a lawsuit. Who knows, they might want to settle with you. Answer B makes no sense, but, hey, that's the law. Answer A, poor Meg Ryan you say. Perhaps you have forgotten about that movie she made with Tom Hanks. Nonetheless, she owns the shop around the corner and somehow "probable cause" (whatever that is) can be found to implicate her, so sue her. Give yourself 300 points. Yes, I know what I said above, but forget it. You deserve 300 points. You'll never get the other questions right anyway.

2. Answer D, obviously. Answer A would be the

answer if you weren't buying a book about humor in the law. Answer E is close, but on appeal it was overturned. Answer C makes no sense. Hopefully you took the extra points from question 1. Don't even think about answer B.

3. Ha ha. That was a tough question, wasn't it? What do you mean it wasn't a question? Okay, stop complaining. The correct answer is E Judge's hand. Fooled you. You thought answer E was simply copied from question 2. The really wrong answer is A, because in the law everything is a question. The rest of the answers are things you might hear in a court and are therefore admissible.

4. Like all reading comprehension questions, you either read it or not. Yes, I now that's a misplaced modifier and that you are not a reading comprehension question. You are a person or a corporate entity. Nonetheless, you know I meant that as in all reading comprehension questions, the *reading* that needs to be comprehended was either read by you or it wasn't. Damn, now that's passive voice. Grammar, go figure. Anyway, you might be interested in the correct answer by now. Answer C is the correct response. Answer A is not the right answer. Don't choose answer A. If you are choosing answer A, you might need to rethink the idea of going to law school. Law school does not give you knowledge of

how to kill people but only knowledge how to make them go broke and want to kill themselves. Answer B would be more realistic but is not in the reading. Answer D is unrealistic since Alice seems to prefer fat guys. If you checked Answer E, then your imagination is running on overtime.

5. Answers A though D could possibly be the correct answer. You will have to look deeply into your own heart and soul to determine which. Don't take too long for that introspection. Answer E might be right, too, but it would be quite a strange answer. On appeal, forget about the judge's hand.

Total up the number of points you have and if they total zero or more, then you can proceed to the next chapter. If you got less than zero points, add 300 to your total and then proceed to the next chapter.

Chapter 1 Take-Aways

Before you read chapter two, make sure you take away the following points from this chapter.

1. This book is for anyone who ever heard of the law (except when Sylvester Stallone, in the movie Judge Dredd, said "I am the law" because that statement made no sense — legally).

2. Taking up law as a profession is not a proper *get rich quick* scheme.

3. There is more to legal humor than dumb stories about lawyers drafting wills for people leaving their life's wealth to their cat.

Lawyers and Pop Culture

There has been so much media hype as to how glamorous the law is. We see lawyers on TV. Not just as commentators on the "news" but also as characters on TV shows.

The realism of TV shows cannot be called into question, especially when Captain Kirk himself, William Shatner, turns out to be one of the most popular TV lawyers.

This book will not bust the hype wide open and expose the reality. No one wants to hear the reality (which involves things like spending your vacation in the hospital and writing memos at 3 o'clock in the morning).

We hear of the big salaries that certain lawyers get, but we don't hear about the myriad attorneys working on temporary document production projects. We hear a lot of Harvard but very little about graduates of small, unaccredited law schools who struggle for decades to pay back their student loans.

We all hear a lot of things. But I won't be discussing them seriously.

Legal Misperceptions

Instead of hearing a lot of things, I've put things into the written word so that you have to read them, not hear them (unless this is the audio book version). Please read the way a normal human being reads, proceeding from the *Introduction* (hereinafter called "the Introduction") through the chapters and to the end. If you didn't read the *Introduction*, go back and read it now, please. I won't bother to suggest that you read the Preface, because that would be going to far

Note that in the last paragraph I did that parenthesis thing with the interior quotes. A lawyer is expected not only to read stuff like that but also to write it, even to think it.[2]

Lawyers also go on and on with damn flowery and barely understandable legal double-talk. It is quite painful. An example is that *hereinafter* and *party of the first part* crap, which causes ulcers better than any microbe.[3]

How can anyone's advice be any simpler: you don't want to be thinking or speaking in those ways! However, if you become a lawyer, sometimes not hearing it can be equally nerve-wracking.

---

[2] The original word used was not *stuff*. A stronger word was deleted.

[3] See discussion of *Stress* in the Conclusion.

Envisioning the law

For example, I had to stop watching *Ally McBeal* because it wasn't following the law. Although the lead character was neurotic and too thin (exactly my type), the deviation from legal precedent was just too much and the whole show was just too unrealistic. Even *Boston Legal*, with my hero Captain Kirk (I mean of course the wonderful actor William Shatner) is sometimes too difficult to watch because it does not reflect a typical law firm.

In a typical law firm there are a lot more blatant illegal activities. Just kidding. Of course I am; this is a humor book. Lot's of kidding. Please remember that it's all a joke.

I even find myself yelling at the TV screen when *Law & Order* (the original series, as I don't have time for spin-offs) is on because invariably they take some obvious point of law (obvious to lawyers) and play it up like it's a big deal.

Disclaimer: I love *Law & Order* and it always accurately applies the law of the land; Sam Waterston is really fantastic and I hope that they put *Oppenheimer*, a show about the creator of the atomic bomb starring Sam in the lead role, on dvd soon because there is nothing but crap on TV, except for, of course *Law & Order* (and what about that first season of *Lost*, or the new *Battlestar Galactica*, and I saw *CSI* for the first time the other night and it wasn't too bad either, and I hear that *The Office* is quite good, though I've never seen it; I'm still bummed Fox canceled *Firefly*). By the way, William Shatner won an Emmy, so I'm not the only person who thinks he's a great actor.

Hollywood Reality

When I first got to law school, I was immediately confronted with the difference between TV/movie law and real life law.

My first day at law school was actually the week before classes began. We had a big welcoming luncheon and I had no idea what I was getting myself into. As would-be lawyers, a little knowledge of the law might be appropriate prior to law school. However, nothing will prepare you in advance.

As it was a hot summer day in August, my choice of wearing shorts might have seemed logical to me in the morning, but as we were finding our seats and I found out where I was sitting, my idiocy became more and more apparent. I had the pleasure of sitting at the Dean's table (I had a scholarship to attend law school and I figure that is why I got seated next to the Dean, but who knows). There were also a few alumni there.

Hint: don't wear shorts to the welcoming luncheon especially if you will be sitting next to the Dean. And, since you might not know if you will be sitting next to the Dean until it is too late, just skip the shorts and dress up a little better.

When the Dean and the alums started discussing the movie *The Verdict*, I thought, since I had seen the movie, that I could offer my opinion. In *The Verdict*, Paul Newman plays Frank Galvin, a drunk, ambulance-chasing lawyer who takes on a medical malpractice case that all the parties want to settle out of court. After displaying his incompetence, the lawyer finally decides to take the case to court to avenge the wrongs inflicted on his client.

I thought it was a pretty good movie and it seems to get pretty good ratings on the various databases. Those databases weren't around the day this movie was discussed at a table with lawyers, wannabe lawyers, and me in shorts.

Just when I was about to say that I liked the movie, I was thankfully cut off by one of the alums. He thought it was terrible. Terrible.

The Dean agreed.

First, Galvin had no right to take the case to trial if his client wanted to settle. Doing so violates all sorts of ethical cannons of the legal profession. It's like a doctor operating on a patient after the patient has said he wants to try drug therapy first. The attorney can't just hijack the case like that.

That was the start. In good lawyer-like form, the Dean and the alums proceeded to pick apart the film scene by scene. They just didn't dislike the movie; they hated it. It was an affront to the legal profession. How could they even make movie like that!

Wow, that's a lot of vitriol for a movie the critics and the public at large (and one shorts-wearing entering-law-student) liked.

Since that day till this day, I still can't watch *The Verdict*. It comes on TV once in a while and all I hear in my head are the voices of the Dean and the alumni berating the film.

Not only do I hear their voices, I echo them now.

I can't enjoy many legal dramas because they take too many liberties. As I mentioned, it got so bad that when *Ally McBeal* was on TV, that I was only able to watch part of the first season before I had to turn off the TV because I just couldn't handle how off they were in terms of following the law. The lead actress could be as thin and neurotic as possible and I still could not handle the show.

On the one hand, you might think that movies and TV shows shouldn't be made if they don't follow the law or legal ethical codes. If you think this, then you are already thinking like a lawyer. In fact, too much like a lawyer.

As I recall (remember I haven't seen *the Verdict* in over 20 years now), the whole dilemma in *the Verdict* was having Galvin overcome his own inequities to win one for the underdog. A sane, rational person would say that's good movie making.

The *Ally McBeal* television series was quite entertaining.

What I am warning against is the inevitable picking apart that you will do with these types of television shows and movies. Being limited like this is not good.

Too much knowledge
is not necessarily a good thing.

David Letterman did a segment many years ago where he would bring on workers in a certain field and have them criticize movies. I particularly remember a welder criticizing *Flash Dance*. He was critical of the woman's long hair, the welding torch flame, and a bunch of other nitpicky welding things.

As a lawyer, you will become hypercritical for a living. And so, you won't be a welder saying that some woman's hair is too long and let it go. You will be quoting OSHA rules in your head and wondering how the building codes are violated.

When you see a movie about the law it will be even worse. It will be like a smorgasbord of technical difficulties laid at your feet. You'll go out of your way to point out to your non-lawyer friends what exactly was wrong with the movie.[4]

Avoiding movies about the law
may be the only way to keep
your non-lawyer friends.

My advice is to keep your friends, especially those non-lawyer friends, and just avoid those movies about the law.

---

[4] This only applies if you have any non-lawyer friends left by the time you get out of law school.

When they call, you answer that you just can't make it because you are too busy. As a lawyer, you will always presumptively be too busy.

If you are right outside the movie theater, and your friends say, "hey, I heard this movie about the law is not only critically acclaimed but is actually a good movie," you will be hard-pressed to tell them that you are too busy to go into the theater with them. Your first instinct as a lawyer might be to say bad things about the movie or criticize the critics. But then you will worry about defamation lawsuits. Instead, improvise. Pretend that you get a phone call (your cell phone is set on vibrate) and that you have to go back to the office because you are a lawyer and you are very busy.

If your phone happens to ring while you are making your pretend phone call, then you are sunk. Sorry. You will have to see the movie. On the bright side, the critics liked it and it supposedly is a good movie.

You might also have to see the movie if your spouse suspects you of having an affair because if you suddenly get a phony phone call, you could be in for far worse consequences than simply sitting through a movie about the law.

There also may be other reasons to see the movie. So, go ahead, see the film. Buy some popcorn (buttered and salted, please), a soda, and maybe those little chocolates with the white sprinkles on top. Other snacks are optional. Please use the trash receptacle after the film is over and exit through the designated doors.

Just don't start talking about the movie either while it is

being shown or anytime thereafter. You will spoil it for everyone if you say anything. Don't say anything.

Your lawyer-nature will stir *objections* within you. After the movie, your friends will be sitting around a table, having some beers and really greasy fried food, laughing and analyzing the movie. You, the lawyer, will be thinking how stupid it all was. Your brain will say that no one could possibly think that anyone who actually knows the law had anything to do with that movie. Stop those brainwaves from getting out of your mouth.

Don't interrupt your friends. Don't point out how stupid it all was. Don't point out that the law cited in the film was wrongly cited, not really a law, or only applicable in Holland. You *objections* will not be welcome.

If you see the movie with a bunch of other lawyers, sure, then you can have fun. You can rip the film to shreds. In fact, it will be a race to see which of you can find the most flaws. One-upping each other will be a great game for the evening.

You can tell them that only Holland has that law on the books.

Also, while you are having those beers and greasy foodstuffs, talk loudly. By doing that, you will impart knowledge to others in the vicinity as to what the law really is. You can express outrage that Hollywood could make such an unrealistic film. And you can appear brilliant in public knowing that Holland might have some strange laws.

Don't worry about ruining the crowd's appreciation of the movie. You are a lawyer and sometimes you have to give people bad news. Besides, these people aren't your friends, you'll never see them again, and even if you do, they know you could sue them for any little thing.

Thus, I have spelled out the options for lawyers. But what if you aren't a lawyer?

If you're not a lawyer, you probably enjoy life a little more and maybe you are not too busy to see a movie that the critics and the public both like. Enjoy the film.

Get that bigger popcorn. Go ahead, indulge.

As you enjoy the film and your extra large popcorn, please remember this (even if it seems unbelievable), that the practice of law is not as glamorous as portrayed on TV or in the movies, involves an awful lot more arguing, and might not accurately state what the law is.

In fact, you might be so tempted by the glamour of the law, that you will go right out of the theatre, go online and download law school applications. When *L.A. Law* was being telecast so many years ago, the number of people applying to law school greatly increased, so I'm not too far off the mark here.

I have to admit, that before I went to law school, I watched repeats of *Perry Mason* (in black & white). I was amazed at how just a couple of questions, a private detective on your payroll, and some quick legal thinking in the middle of the speediest trial you will ever see, will get you a verdict of innocent.

Perry Mason never had any paperwork.
Your legal practice will have a lot.

No paperwork. No long hours. No motions to extend the trial by 600 days. Just a bunch of questions, a trial, and you're home free.

Some witness on the stand will start to cry and admit to being the killer. Some guy in the back of the court will yell that he is the real murderer.

Amazing. But true?

In all my years of practice, I have never seen a representative of an insurance company stand up in the back of the court and yell out that his insurance company was liable.

No corporate president ever broke down on the witness stand at the trial of his competitor and confessed that it was his company that really built the faulty machine.

There was never any warm embrace at the end of a patent dispute where the two sides hug each other, sobbing, with the one company president telling the other company president, "I know you could never infringe on our patents."

**Unlike in *Perry Mason*, in real life
no insurance company representative
will ever stand up in the back of the courtroom
and admit that his insurance company
is liable and should pay.**

Hollywood and the law don't seem to mix. And if you see that incredible movie about the law and run to get a law school application in the mail, you may only see a lot later that taking up the law as a profession is not all it's cracked up to be.

Remember that what they have up on the big screen or what they have on the little screen (that's TV) usually isn't too accurate except what is on *Law & Order* and anything William Shatner does because I went to law school with his daughter, I've met him, and he's a really nice guy. Funny, too.

Quiz concerning lawyers and pop culture

1. William Shatner is to Sam Waterston as

    a. Denny Crane is to whomever Sam Waterston plays on *Law & Order*.

    b. Captain James T. Kirk of the Starship Enterprise is to the Lonely Squire of Gothos.

    c. Patrick Stewart is to Leonard Nimoy.

    d. Fluffernutter is to organic and, most likely sugar-free, peanut butter.

    e. one TV lawyer is to another TV lawyer.

2. Law school alumni have odd opinions about popular and critically acclaimed movies because

    a. they have been to law school and it warped their minds.

    b. law schools only accept people who don't like popular movies.

    c. as lawyers, they like to argue for no good reason, and this results in always pointing out what was wrong in a movie you really liked so you can't enjoy it anymore.

    d. the free lunch they are served at alumni functions tastes weird.

    e. it is written into the professional ethics code that they must have weird opinions.

3. Of the following possible answers, which TV character is your favorite legal idol?

    a. Doc from *Gunsmoke*.

    b. Hawkeye from *MASH*.

    c. Dr. Ben Casey from some really old doctor show.

    d. The Blues Brothers.

    e. Denny Crane.

4. This is the dreaded reading comprehension question. Don't go back and read the chapter now. Besides, it's either a lot of blah blah blah about nothingness or information that could save your life. Either way it's too late to go back and read it now. Don't ask why it is too late, as it will make your brain hurt. Oh, yes, the question (I almost forgot). Based on the information is this chapter, what shouldn't you wear to a lunch with the law school Dean?

    a. A really really tight bathing suit.

    b. Shorts.

    c. Tights.

    d. A top-hat.

    e. Lacy stuff.

5. Why is there no mention of the movie (or the TV spin-off of the movie) *The Paper Chase*?

    a. The what?

    b. In the movie, the action supposedly takes place at Harvard, but the film was shot at the University of Southern California in Los Angeles, so the whole movie is a crock to begin with. Why couldn't they have simply said that the action was taking place at the University of Southern California? Because they're snobs.

c.   There is no mention of it because no one cares.

d.   There is no mention of it because no one remembers that movie.

e.   The stupid movie with John Houseman barking at students! How thrilling! Why did they call the movie that?

Quiz Answers

Questions deserve answers even if they were really bad questions.

1.   If you were tricked into answering Answer A, then you were tricked. It's not A; definitely not A. Don't argue. You have to follow the mood of the test. That's what they tell you when you are taking the SAT, the LSAT, the bar exam, and every other test that has seemingly dopey answers to simple questions. It's the same here. The reason that A is wrong is because William Shatner also played other lawyers. Once he played a lawyer in some obscure movie around 40 years ago about the trial of the camp commandant of a Confederate prison who was accused of war crimes and then executed. I think Richard Basehardt played the camp commandant. The importance of that trial was that it was the first time that someone was found guilty of war crimes even though he was a soldier and following orders. At least it was the first time a TV movie had been made about such an incident that didn't involve World War II. So answer E actually fits better because William Shatner shouldn't only be known for one character he played. He also played T.J. Hooker, but that was a cop and not a lawyer and so if you were answering E to Question 1 and you were thinking that I meant *T.J. Hooker*, then you should

be marked wrong even though you got the answer correct. However, since you answered correctly and this isn't a *show your work* type quiz, I guess you can get credit for your answer. You have been warned, though. As for Sam Waterston, he has played a number of other roles on TV and in the movies but space limitations preclude me from rambling aimlessly about them here. Oh, yes, the other choices are wrong. B comes close except that you have to have a lot of extra *Star Trek* knowledge but even then Sam Waterston is not the child of interstellar super-beings nor ever played one on TV. C is wrong because a comparison between a captain in Picard's century to a Vulcan who was never captain of the ship with the same name wouldn't seem right. D is admittedly close, but you'll notice that I didn't include Nutella or any chocolate-hazelnut spread.

2. The answer is A. This time A is not the trick response. The other answers are wrong answers to the question even though they are true. You'll recall that nitpicky distinction between a correct answer and an incorrect but true answer from the SAT. It is still a ridiculous distinction but I'm using it here.

3. What a giveaway! A real freebee. Of course the answer is E. No, not because William Shatner plays Denny Crane on the show *Boston Legal*. I can't even

believe that you thought I would make a pointless question just to highlight how great William Shatner is. All the other answers are characters who were not lawyers. Look, let's face it. I really have no idea who your favorite legal idol is, especially on TV. Maybe you like Fred Thompson. Maybe you are a legal groupie. Perhaps you collect cases of your favorite lawyer. Maybe you also eat grubs that live in mud in some far-off muddy plain. Where you get your grubs from is not important. As it is on the bar exam or in the courtroom, what is important is that you get the right answer.

4. Goodness gracious! You shouldn't wear any of those things. However, you'll notice that there is no *all the above* answer. I'm not going to explain the answer here. Why didn't you do the assigned reading? If you are called on in class, you will really be destroyed — a bad fate. The correct answer is B.

5. The movie *The Paper Chase* isn't mentioned in this chapter, not because no one remembers, since I'm sure one of you actually does remember the film, but rather because no one cares. Answer C. If you got this question right, then tell yourself that you have "earned it", which is what John Houseman used to say in some commercial for some investment company and I am explaining it *ad nauseam* here because not too many people remember. However, I

probably shouldn't have explained that last sentence because no one cares. Answer C again.

Chapter 2 Take-Aways

Below are some really important things you should have learned from reading Chapter 2. Basically, if you didn't read Chapter 2, here's what you missed

1. Know where you will be sitting at all law school luncheons and dress appropriately.

2. *The Verdict* is a movie that starred some guy who makes salad dressing.

3. The female lead in the TV show *Ally McBeal* was thin.

4. The author likes *Star Trek*.

5. Attending law school will inhibit your ability to enjoy a lot of films and TV shows.

6. *Perry Mason*'s lack of paperwork, ability to get confessions from guilty parties (not his client), and speedy court system are fictional and should never be confused with the real life practice of law.

Pre-Law Fallacies

What most lawyers fail to realize is that they are not as important as doctors. Doctors, at least the vast majority who aren't killing people *Doctor Kevorkian* style, are in the business of saving lives.

Lawyers, on the other hand, are in the business of arguing. It does not even matter if there is no point to the argument, they still argue. They argue whether their client, who was injured by a meteorite, can sue the big oil companies for not using minerals from space instead of crude bubbling up from the ground. Put together a really tough jury in California and you have a case.

While many lawsuits are noble causes, few get to the same degree of nobility as emergency surgery to remove that ax from the brain of a lumberjack.

Do not start defending lawyers in your mind or your brain will start to hurt more than if you had an ax stuck in it. Please note that I'm conjuring up imagery here because the brain actually doesn't feel any pain in itself, though the entry of the ax through the skull would cause some discomfiture.

Law is not medicine.

As lawyers we're not saving anyone's life here. Still most lawyers act as if it's all life and death if we don't file this legal brief with the court on time, which it isn't.[5]

Law is about arguing over issues and convincing people that you have it right. It is about winning. Medicine is about curing people or, at the fringe, making up diseases.

Is there a need for political scientists?

I had had a choice. I was not a political science major in college. If you are a political science major right now, my best advice would be to get out while you still can — even if you need an extra year of college. Because a person who majors in political science is almost condemned to go to law school.

What else would you do?

There are not too many job ads calling for political scientists. Besides the fact that there is little science to politics, there is little else to do after graduation than to contemplate more school.

The salesperson who sold me my first Volkswagen was a political science major. He had expected to do things with

---

[5] Death penalty states excluded.

his undergraduate education besides selling Volkswagens. The car he sold me was the floor model so it had been slightly used, so my political science salesman was a used car salesman.[6]

I'm not saying that everyone who majors in political science will become a used car salesperson. Many would be lucky to sell used cars. Many others would go into a deep depression. I am merely suggesting that the odds of you becoming a used car salesperson are far greater than you being called up to work for the US State Department.

If you are studying political science, really look at your career potential once you leave the lovely confines of your college. You will either have to do well on the Foreign Service exam, be connected to some politicos, or get a Masters degree or PhD. Those are the options if you want to go into political science.

However, many people take political science because it sounds more current that History, more prestigious than Sociology, less tedious than English, and less math than Business. Forget about what you think about the other fields. At least they lead to jobs.

As I said, though, I wasn't a political science major, so I had a choice. I was an electrical engineer. In the distant past, when Americans actually built things, getting a degree in engineering was not a far-fetched concept. You might ask

---

[6] And I got it for several thousand dollars cheaper – just thought you should know. Nowadays they would call it pre-owned and charge a premium.

how an electrical engineer becomes a lawyer. Working in the defense industry is enough to warp anyone's sense of reality.

As I sat in my cubicle (I can't even say *my cubicle* because the cubicles held 4 people, the walls were eye level high from a sitting position — so it was more like a great hall of desks) next to 65-year-old Irving, I got so depressed I almost got an ulcer. What was getting me depressed was not Irv nor that he was 65. The problem was that at 22, I saw my whole life in front of me. From 22 to 65, I would move one desk over. And my desk was in a better location than Irv's.[7]

In the midst of this depressional onset, I noticed a group of men in suits walking by. Who were they? They had the fancy offices, private secretaries, and were located in the fancier part of the building. Cubicles for them? Hardly. They had their own offices with walls up to the ceiling. They were the lawyers, of course. Their starting salary was more than Irv was making with 25 years as an engineer at the firm. They negotiated the contracts that we used to build the warship I was working on. To top it all off — this being the indignity of the situation — the contract was poorly written and mandated engineering that was out-of-date.

To summarize: treated like kings in the corporate world, yet they wrote crap. For that they made three times the money I was making as an engineer. The only impediments

---

[7] I'd have to wait to law school for the actual ulcer, but that had more to do with my law student/law student relationship than with torts or contracts. See Chapter 15 for relationship advice to help prevent relationship-induced ulcers.

were 3 years of my life, lots of money spent, and tons of added stress — and that's only law school. Then there's the bar exam, associate life at law firms, and many other detriments I hadn't considered.

Thus, not considering any of these negatives, it was off the law school I went, to one of the top 20 that gave me a scholarship. I thought my life would become one of those Hollywood fantasies come true (a job fantasy, not some other impossible Hollywood fantasy). My new reality was soon to come front and center.

Quiz concerning pre-law fallacies

1. Why was this chapter so short?
   a. There's not much to say.
   b. A college major in political science will get you a fascinating job — the end.
   c. Because in the final debate, who makes more money, doctors or lawyers, will never be settled, so why drone on about it here.
   d. To give the reader (you) a break.
   e. None of the above.

2. What are your career options if your college major is political science?
   a. Used car sales.
   b. Hollywood fantasies.
   c. Political scientist.
   d. Ambassador.
   e. More school.

3. Based on the reading, match the field of interest to the reason why majoring in political science might be preferable:

History	more prestigious
Sociology	less math
English	more current
Business	less tedious
Engineering	not yet obsolete

Quiz Answers

If you go to law school, you might have your final grade in each class depends on your score on only one test, the final. That is a pretty nasty situation to be in. Some new-fangled professors might grade you on class participation or on how you answer questions on cases discussed in class. However, few will give you quizzes to gage your progress. In this book, quizzes are given in the hope that they will better prepare you for understanding the law. And if you believe that, then I have a bridge in the middle of the desert that needs a buyer and you look to be it.

1. E, none of the above, is the correct answer. A is wrong because there is probably a lot more to say on the subject, I just can't bother now. B is wrong because Political Science is not all that fascinating. It might be interesting, but fascinating takes it way too far. C is wrong because the debate has been settled. D is wrong because if anyone is getting a break, it will be me.

2. This could almost be a trick question because there might not be an answer to this question. Let's be nice and agree that the correct answer is C, political scientist. But is that really a career?

3. This quiz was soooooo damn easy. You should be so lucky to get an easy quiz while in law school. The

study of political science supposedly is more current than history, more prestigious than sociology, less tedious than English, less math than business, and not yet obsolete like engineering. Yes, law might have less math than engineering, but, as always, we are looking for the best answers here. If fact, all we are interested in is the right answer. The law is a noble profession looking for truth and justice (the *American way* was deleted because the society on planet Sigma Draconus 4 has a more pure way that connects with the infinite forces of the universe). Actually, the law isn't that noble and is more likely concerned with expediency (and Sigma Draconus 4 doesn't have a better way because there's no advanced society there).

Chapter 3 Take-Aways

Chapter 3 was really short because I thought it would be less taxing for you to have a short chapter you could read in the bathroom and dispatch quickly. Hopefully you took your own book into your own bathroom. Taking someone else's book into your bathroom or taking your book into someone else's bathroom are not advised.

Anyway, this is what you would have gleaned from Chapter 3, had you read it.

1. The Mayan calendar ends on December 21, 2012, so plan your life accordingly.

2. There is no advanced society on Sigma Draconus 4.

3. Take political science as a college major and you might end up selling used Volkswagens.

4. Consider studying medicine instead of law.

4

The Art of Arguing and the Science of Nitpicking

Argumentation is at the heart of the law. We know from Newton or some other physicist (or from your physics professor, if you even had a class in physics), that an object in motion tends to stay in motion. Court is a place where two opposing objects are in motion. When those two opposing objects hit, all that kinetic energy is converted into heat, as in an explosion, as in an explosion in your stomach, which we can refer to as an ulcer.

Sure, sure, ulcers can be caused by microbes, but they can also be caused by stress. And if you see fit to argue that point, then I suggest you do a little experimentation. Go to law school, take the bar exam, work at a law firm, and you will have your own study in gastro-intestinal distress.

There is no more distressing place to be than in the

bathroom of a prominent New York City law firm listening to the lilting tones of lawyers emptying their bowels.

Disgusting? Perhaps, but also it is reality.

If you can escape being a lawyer, do so at your earliest possible convenience. It's not that the practice of law isn't fun and exciting, nor is it the fact that it is a lot of hard work, stress, and ...

Wait a minute!

Fun? Actually, it isn't really all that fun.

Excitement?

Waiting for that next fax from the court telling you that your motion has been denied can be exciting. Sitting in a deposition when your client says something self-incriminating can be exciting. However, not the kind of excitement like participating in the extreme sport of walking down the side of a building in Auckland, New Zealand. It's more like the excitement of failing music class in junior high school and realizing that your academic record will be permanently scarred.

Of course I don't know you personally. You might thrive on stress — we're talking about thriving on the *failing music class* type of stress not the *extreme sports* type. Or, you might be one of the lucky ones who bounces from one good thing to the next.[8]

When I refer to *you*, I am referring to the reader who didn't get into the top school but only into one of the top

---

[8] Bouncing like a basketball rebound not like Tigger from *Winnie the Pooh* – because Tigger is unique.

twenty.[9]

You might also be someone who is mildly unhappy in your present job and doesn't realize that you will be extremely unhappy as a lawyer. I am especially referring to all those paralegals who think they should go to law school after spending years seeing the misery that most lawyers are in on a daily basis yet thinking, erroneously, that since the lawyers are making more money, they must be happier than they seem to be.

They're not.

Arguing for the sake of arguing

Lawyers and people who want to become lawyers sometimes have this odd knack of wanting to argue about things. Arguing when there is no need to argue.

I had this problem once on a date — I'm referring to arguments not worthy of trial.

I met this incredibly hot woman on one of those internet dating sites and we had gone out a couple of times. While walking her back to her place in Brooklyn from a party we had attended, we were discussing relationships. I suggested that a good relationship needed two things, both chemistry and compatibility. By chemistry, I meant that spark that makes you fall in love. Anyway, the more I tried to define chemistry or the spark, the more questions she asked, until I had had enough and refused to answer anymore questions.

---

[9] Woe to thee who only gets into an unaccredited institution.

Feeling that she had won some sort of match, she told me that my arguments would never hold up in court.

She was, of course, a law student being on that outer edge of annoying that many law students become: arguing just for the sake of arguing. For many lawyers, arguing for the sake of arguing is just natural (not second nature, but first nature) and that makes them annoying.

Now, don't get me wrong. I love to argue, too.

But arguing over nothing can be a bit extreme.

Spark, chemistry – you get it, right?

Plus, it was 5 a.m. and I was walking her home, which was 3 hours out of my way!

To reiterate: she was arguing just for the sake of arguing.

And my arguments would have held up in court (if I had a supportive judge).

Nitpicking things and people to death

Nitpicking things to death doesn't stop with ripping movies to shreds (as described in an earlier chapter). When it translates into your real life — watch out. The divorce rate among lawyers and their spouses, I would venture, is directly proportional to the nitpickiness of the attorney-spouse.

Nitpicking can be bad for any of your relationships. At the end of my first semester of first year law school, I was back at my parent's home for Christmas. My younger brother, a whiz at writing computer programs wrote a whopper — a very impressive program. He brings it over to me, who, though an electrical engineer, could read his program but never could have written it. So he shows me the program. What was the first thing I said? "You have a mistake on line 42."

Let's review. My brother writes a fantastic computer program and the first thing I do is find some minor mistake and point it out to him. What a nice brother, not.

My brother takes the page, sees the errors, and thanks me. He thanks me! Eegahd!

As he returned to his room, I realized what I had done. Years later when I was president of my law school's Student Bar Association, I shared that story with incoming first year students so that they might realize when law school turns them into jerks. Hopefully they could redeem themselves before it was too late. The rule: don't be a jerk.

I followed my brother into his room and told him what a wonder program he wrote. Being a stand-up kind of guy, he said thanks but that he had made a mistake.

We all make mistakes. When practicing law, it's good to point out the other side's mistakes. In real life, though, pointing out someone's mistake is not always appropriate. I should have first told my brother that he had a wonderful program. Maybe later after looking at it longer, I could have mentioned the mistake. The praise was the important thing. The nitpicking was simply nitpicking.

The first semester of the first year law school will turn you into a nitpicker. If you really want to be an effective lawyer, then learn your nitpicking well. However, if you want to be an effective human being, know when to turn the nitpicking off. Since the switch is hidden in your brain, you'll have to use judgment.

Actual nitpicks include the following:

1. A man telling a beautiful woman who is wearing a very sexy dress that exposes her midriff that she needs to tighten up her abs a bit.

2. A woman telling a man who she was interested in that his gut needs to hang over his belt a bit more.

Those are actual nitpicks — do not use them. Although they might be true, there is no need to nitpick to that extent. A typical nitpick could look like this scene below:

As you can see, nitpicking could mean that you don't

discover where Atlantis is. It could also alienate people from evening trying to discover Atlantis or, more realistically, help with the Johnson case.

Of course nitpicking can be fun, but getting your fun from nitpicking is like going over to the Dark Side.

The force might be strong; you could be strolling into court in a swanky black cape and sounding like James Earl Jones as your make your statement to the jury. However, in the end you'll probably wind up in an odd helmet-mask wheezing about Luke Skywalker's paternity issues.

Let's see how dangerous arguing, nitpicking, and other stressors can be. As you see from the scientifically produced chart below, the Dark Side can take its toll on you.

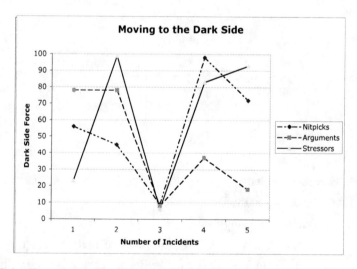

This first chart shows how incidents of nitpicks etc. will draw you to the Dark Side. For some reason, studies indicate that at 3 nitpicks, arguments or stressors, the Dark Side force is low but that is probably because you have to defend yourself from the Dark Side. That's what current scientific theory says.

However, you can see from the second scientifically produced chart, below, that when you cause the evil, there is a steady increase in the Dark Side force. And the more you increase that Dark Side force, the more you risk being stuck on a Death Star with an evil emperor.

Compare the chart on the previous page with the one below. Amazing how scientific they both are.

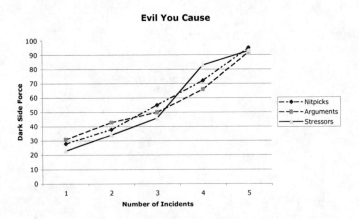

This second chart shows conclusively that if you are bad you will be drawn to the Dark Side.

What am I trying to say?

I think it has to do with the faces of the women in my drawing a couple of pages back. If you nitpick, you start to look quite hideous.[10]

---

[10] I drew badly on purpose.

There is that story about the guy who never got old but his picture got old.[11]

In contrast to that fictitious story, nitpickers get ugly – ugly souls (not their pictures).

The moral of this chapter is that lawyers can be as *Dark Side* as they want to be in court — but when you leave the courtroom, you should leave the Dark Side behind.

Therefore, go and sin no more.

---

[11] In *The Picture of Dorian Gray* by Oscar Wilde, a classic gothic horror fiction story that details how bad acts affect the soul.

Quiz concerning the art of arguing, etc.

1. If you nitpick, you are likely to
    a. join the Dark Side.
    b. get uglier with each nitpick.
    c. be shot by Bruce Willis, as in one of those *Die Hard* movies.
    d. lose friends and alienate family.
    e. breathe heavily and talk like James Earl Jones.

2. Now for the reading comprehension question. Where did my brother make a mistake on his computer program?
    a. On Line 42
    b. On Line 18
    c. On the conga line.
    d. Online.
    e. On the bottom line.

3. What would be the best caption for the picture of the two women in this chapter?
    a. Ugly women debate the merits of Plato's description of Atlantis and the Johnson case.
    b. Dora Gray, evil nitpicker.
    c. Another episode of *Histories Mysteries* focuses on the Johnson case.
    d. An artist's rendition of nitpicking in a major law firm (although "artist" is questionable).

     e.   Pirates attack Atlantic shipping.

4. Which activity, from the ones listed below, would be the most fun?

     a.   Failing music class.

     b.   Jumping from a building in Auckland, New Zealand.

     c.   Going to the bathroom in a big New York City law firm.

     d.   Getting a divorce.

     e.   Working with microbes.

5. A courtroom is to an explosion as

     a.   nitpicking is to an attorney.

     b.   your stomach is to an ulcer.

     c.   James Earl Jones is to Bruce Willis.

     d.   a learned hand is to Judge Learned Hand (yes, there really was a famous Judge named Learned Hand).

     e.   stress is the to Dark Side.

Quiz Answers

If you have gotten this far into the book and are still taking the quizzes, give yourself 100 points. Heck, give yourself 200 points (I have points to spare).

1. Bruce Willis may or may not shoot you. You might have valuable information that he could use or you might be so despicable that he will have no choice but to shoot you, so answer C isn't correct. Besides, even if he does shoot you, he might not shoot you like in one of those *Die Hard* movies. Answer E is wrong because sounding like James Earl Jones could be a very good thing. Answer A is wrong as we see in the 3rd incident rule from the first graph in this chapter. Answer B only makes sense for the graphic novel version of your life. If you nitpick you are likely to alienate friends and family, so answer D is the correct answer.

2. Answer C would only make sense if he gave me the computer program during a wedding. Answer D is the computer geek answer and answer E is the MBA response. Both are wrong; terribly wrong. Answer B is the trick answer. For those of you who were good enough to actually read the chapter or my brother's computer program, you will clearly see that answer A is the correct response.

3. Answer A is close, but it doesn't get to the heart of the matter. Don't forget that the question asked for the best answer not the second best answer. Answer B is wrong because Dora is the explorer not an evil nitpicker. Answer E is wrong because pirates don't nitpick they pillage and plunder. Pirates can be irritating to shipping but they're not really nitpickers. Answer D is correct because that's what the picture is.

4. Although, it's not quite as bad as failing art class, failing music class in any grade is not fun. Thus, answer A is wrong. Answer B is the trick response, because I say jumping off a building in Auckland, not climbing down it or bungee jumping from it. Jumping off most any building from greater than 5 stories will kill you and, in most likelihood, jumping from smaller buildings could leave you paralyzed. Death or paralysis are not normally considered the end products of fun activities, so if you answered B to this question, either you were tricked or you need some serious counseling. Stop watching shows like *Fear Factor* for a start. And stay away from those damn rollerblades. No matter how happy you will be after a divorce, the process of getting a divorce is a painful one, so answer D is wrong. Working with microbes leads to all sorts of violent creatures attacking you (see the SciFi channel for further details), making answer E wrong. Therefore, the

correct answer is C, going to the bathroom in a New York City law firm, because if you wait around for just a few minutes, you will get to hear a cacophony of sounds like post-modernist new age concert. Naturally, once you hear those sounds, you should exit the bathroom immediately or else you will be overcome by toxic fumes. Legal gastrointestinal distress: interesting for the ears but deadly for the nose.

5. The James Earl Jones / Bruce Willis comparison makes no sense. Maybe if you had a Jones-Schwarzenegger-Willis triad, that might be something interesting, but even that makes no sense unless the categories involve fictional characters. Answer C is wrong. Answer D is also wrong because it also makes no sense. Nonetheless, that judge had a very weird name. His parents, though, were never thought to have been in psychotherapy. Nitpicking is something attorneys do, but then again we are looking for the best answer to this question, not just any answer. A and E are wrong. B is the right answer because that is what is on the answer key.

Chapter 4 Take-Aways

There are a lot of things you could take away from this chapter. I can't draw really well. The graphs make no sense. The stories are uninteresting. And the whole nitpicking/arguing/stress thing is a complete over-exaggeration. However, let's focus on the positive take-aways instead; the ones that will make you a better human being and possibly even a better lawyer.

1. Lawyers learn to nitpick, which is good for legal things, but then do damage to their various relationships by nitpicking too much.

2. Avoid the Dark Side in your personal life and reserve those lightsabers for battles with opposing counsel (not for your date).

3. Arguing even when there is no need to argue is not good thing. Save your arguing for court, where it's the right thing to do.

5

One-L

or

How One is the Loneliest Number

(or maybe some other title would be appropriate)

For some odd reason you are proud of yourself because you got into law school. Perhaps you always wanted to know what a tort is. Perhaps you like spending tens of thousands of dollars for the privilege of being made a fool of in contracts class. Perhaps you don't realize how much it will really cost you in the end. Or perhaps someone is paying the bill for you so years of useless academic knowledge don't pose a painful choice.

Perhaps you like watching those Sunday morning political chat-fests on the television news and since every now and then they mention what sounds like a famous court case, you are eager for a class in constitutional law. Whatever your reason, you have arrived. You are on the road to being a lawyer. Prepare to suffer.

You get to suffer for three years, but the first year contains the most suffering. First year students are called "One Ls" – isn't that brilliant! However, no one calls third year students "Three Ls"; they are simply called "Third Years".

Now that you have the hip law school lingo down, let's turn to some examples of suffering that you could be exposed to.

The Case of the Missing Casebooks

The week before law school already contained the germ of an important realization. The first week of classes contains a vastly greater number of germs. Preparing for class, meeting your classmates, and answering in class for the first time provides a plague of novel experiences you'll treasure forever.[12]

The first thing you will realize when you meet your fellow classmates is that law school doesn't conduct interviews as part of the admission process. The colorful personalities you meet will be the same ones that you will be

---

[12] Unless you wise-up and get an MBA instead.

getting coffee with, forming study groups with, and competing with. Just remember the last part. It's not quite like the Roman Empire or the Klingon Empire, but you'll know soon enough whether your school is hyper-competitive or just competitive.

Many law schools are plagued by mysteriously disappearing casebooks. I found myself lucky that my classmates weren't intent on stealing the casebooks everyone would need for their first research class. You might not be so lucky. How do you prepare against having the book that need for your class not vanishing from the law library? Go to business school.

Everyone says that everything has changed because of the internet. Let's pretend that the internet will make up for missing books. It might. It does that pretty well in normal situations. But that might only mask the disease of excessive competitiveness rather than being a cure for it.

Pounding out your first legal memorandum

The best thing about the first semester of first year law school is your introduction to stress. The stress of meeting arbitrary deadlines, where your career hangs in the balance, will be a lesson the dutiful 1L should learn well.

In my class there was a man in his mid thirties who had had his own business, worked for the Olympics, and was very impressive all around. One night while I was working in the law library, this classmate came in and showed me his printout of his first legal memorandum.[13]

The pages of his memo were twisted into what looked like a Chinese dumpling without the filling. The missing filling turned out to be my classmate's fist. He had been pounding the life out of his memo on his bed for the past hour.

Punching your paper doesn't get it written any faster.

It seemed to me that he was experiencing a bit of frustration while attempting to write his first legal memorandum. And, he admitted a bit of frustration at the memo and even more about the first few weeks of law school.

I did the unthinkable. I convinced to stick it out and stay in school, which he did. I know — I'm evil.

Learning to Translate into Legalese

Now don't sit there and think, "oh, it was just a memo and I can write a memo."[14]

Don't think that.

A legal memorandum is not in the same category as the memo you recently got saying that the firm you work for has cut another holiday out of the calendar and is now

---

[13] It was one of almost every night spent in the law library.

[14] But don't read this book while standing.

combining Memorial Day and Labor Day into a new holiday in August called Superintendent's Conference Day. It is not the memo telling the boss that the new computer system doesn't work.

A legal memorandum is a complex set of words arranged on the paper in an obscure dialect of English called *legalese*, which most people will not be able to understand, even if they had a pre-law class in college. Pre-law is about as relevant to the actual study of law as geology. You would have better luck staring at rocks for a few hours than the misguided (though, of course, well-intentioned) "education" that pre-law provides. But enough of my mockery of pre-law, we've got a memo to discuss.

Part of a legal memo might look like the following:

As is well established in the products liability arena, manufacturers need not be in privity for the end users to require a warning. Such a privity discussion is avoided here since it is now largely academic. *Stevens v. Parke, Davis & Co.* (1973) 9 Cal.3d 51; 107 Cal.Rptr. 45 and *Carmichael v. Reitz* (1971) 17 Cal.App.3d 958; 95 Cal.Rptr. 381, are among the cases which recognize that a duty to warn extends to persons not in privity. Furthermore, such a discussion does not facilitate the application of these products liability principles to the construction defect circumstance. *Section 324A of the Restatement (Second) of Torts* permits an individual who is not a party to a contract, but who is within the scope of hazard created by the contract activity, to maintain a cause of action against the contracting party for negligent performance of ...

Fascinating stuff?

If your eyes are glazing over, then join the rest of the human race.

If your eyes have not glazed over, perhaps you need more recent case citations.

And, if you recognized that the citations aren't to Blue Book standards, then you have recently graduated law school and this book was given to you as a gift. Ha, ha. Very funny. It's too late to go to business school as you have student loans to pay back.

If you are lawyer and didn't care whether it was Blue Booked standardly, then either you have been practicing too long to care, you never cared, or you are trying very hard to wonder to what case this memorandum refers. Never mind. It's an old memo. I'm just trying to make a point to the uninitiated that legal writing isn't like the kind of writing most people are used to.

The Blue Book might refer to a condition that parts of the male genitalia develop under certain adverse conditions.

Apply these same conditions to the law and you have the Blue Book. The Blue Book, written by the same people who correct your grammar while speaking, is the standard reference guide as to how legal stuff should be written. Many courts have their own ways of wanting legal stuff written, so the self-proclaimed gods of legal grammar aren't the last word. Nonetheless, you violate their rules at your own risk. Substantial risk.

Imagine being ridiculed for not Blue Booking properly. It is a terrible taunt and your reputation within your law firm will sink rather precipitously.

My example was just a little piece of nonsense from a little memo. Don't make me come up with future examples, especially involving the *Second Restatement of Torts*.

As an aside (which actually is the status of most of this book — one long aside), the *Second Restatement of Torts* should tell you that the first restatement was obviously a load of crap. If you go to law school and find out what a tort is, then you and the *Second Restatement of Torts* will become fast friends. You'll be looking for issues to relate to it and, by Jove, you probably will find them.

By the way, these Restatements are necessary because we are a Common Law country. The common law is not law that is for commoners. Rather, the common law refers to the legal heritage we got from the English where the law has grown over time from the cases that judges have decided. Yep, judges made the law in the past.[15]

---

[15] And still make law today; but no one likes to say that.

Since legal research can turn up old court decisions on any and all sides of any argument, prominent legal scholars thought it would be a good idea to write down what they thought the law should be. The states of the US thought something similar at the end of the 19th century and started codifying all the laws into statutes. That made for a lot of fun.

However, not all the laws are codified. For instance laws of evidence in the state of New York are not codified. Can't find statutes concerning evidence in New York? How do lawyers know what the rules of evidence are in New York? Silly question? They are scattered about in thousands of separate court decisions. Luckily, law book publishers collected all these rules and put them into a book.

But who knows what's real and what isn't? In California, a guy named Bernie Witkin, who failed the California bar exam several times, published a series of books that supposedly compile the rules of law for various topics. These books, oft cited in California courts as *the* authority, were actually Bernie's bar review study notes. Yes, you read that correctly: the guide to California law originated as the study notes from a guy who failed the bar numerous times. I met him many years ago and he seemed like a nice guy, but I'm not too fond of his notes.

Who are these people writing the Restatements? I never saw one but I am sure they are actual people. There is a credible theory that the Restatements were written by aliens from outer space, but the jury is still out on that theory.

There are lots of Restatements and I'm sure there are

crazed lawyers out there in the world just salivating at the idea that some obscure area of law needs a Restatement written. Please do not become one of them!

Quiz concerning One-L

1. Which answer best completes the following statement: If lawyers wrote a *Restatement of Murphy's Law*, it would probably _____

    a. be extremely long and boring.

    b. start with some statement to the effect that anything that can go wrong, will.

    c. restate it so much that it sounds nothing like the original.

    d. would only make sense to lawyers.

    e. be cited in many legal papers.

2. What is Blue Booking?

    a. Being very lonely.

    b. As in "booking" a gig, blue booking is booking a racy or indecent gig.

    c. Turning a book blue.

    d. Making sure your *legalese* dialect is proper.

    e. The process of making a legal memorandum into a work of art.

3. Reading comprehension question. Why was the law student punching his legal memorandum?

    a. To make a strong point.

    b. To give the memo some "punch".

    c. He was angry at the law.

    d. He was frustrated.

    e. He was just simulating punching. He was

really making a Chinese dumpling.

4. What is the best thing about being a 1L?
    a. As a 1L, you don't have to eat vegetables that you really don't like.
    b. You get to spend lots of time in the library; you get to stay up all night.
    c. You learn to speak *legalese*.
    d. It almost validates taking political science as an undergraduate major.
    e. You are probably spending more money than ever did in your whole life.

5. What would have been another title for this chapter?
    a. Your Introduction to *Legalese*
    b. Law is Hell
    c. How Come We Haven't Seen Any Buffalo?
    d. Writing Law Stuff
    e. None of the Above

Quiz Answers

Being a 1L is not easy, like taking a silly quiz. So when you take this quiz, do not think it will actually prepare you for the first year of law school.

1. Murphy's Law states that what can go wrong will. There are many other versions of what that 'law' is but we are not concerned with them here. What we are concerned with is what would happen if a bunch of lawyers got together and started writing a long treatise on the subject. Answer E is not the correct choice because the *Restatement of Murphy's Law* would not really be something that lawyers would put in their legal briefs (unlike underwear, legal briefs are papers filed with a court). As always, we are looking for not just a true answer but the best answer. Answer D would be wrong because it really would not make sense to anyone; lawyers may tell you it makes sense to them, but they would be lying. Answer C is wrong because Restatements of the law are not like playing the game of telephone at a four-year-old's birthday party. Answer B is wrong because you can rest assured that they would never start the thing off with Murphy's law itself – that would be too unlawyerlike. Since we are looking for the best answer, answer A would be the right choice because if lawyers are writing it, it is almost a certainty that it would be long and boring, even to

other lawyers. On the other hand, all the answers sound pretty good, so if you got this question wrong, you can tell people that you actually got it right. Just don't tell me since I want plausible deniability.

2. This was a painful question. The answer is D. The other answers, those that are not D, are wrong. Please don't ask for a whole recitation of why each wrong answer is wrong. Haven't we had enough of that already?

3. The reading comprehension questions are always totally lame. They get really bad when you have to draw a conclusion based on the reading. Luckily for you, you only had to mildly skim this chapter to get it right. He didn't punch his legal memorandum because he was making a Chinese dumpling. It only looked like a Chinese dumpling. So, answer E was wrong and if you picked E, then perhaps you should read more closely. He wasn't angry at the law; rather, he was frustrated being a first year law student (what we referred to in this chapter as being a 1L). So, answer D is the correct answer and answer C is wrong. The other wrong answers are so stupid, that you should not have picked them even if you didn't read the chapter, unless your opinion of the reading material would cause you to answer A or B.

4. The best thing about being a 1L is not answer E,

spending more money than you ever had before, because you are spending that money on law school tuition. Answer A is wrong for two opposite reasons. Either you are always being forced to eat vegetables you don't like or you always have the freedom not to eat vegetables you don't like. Vegetables that people don't like vary from person to person. Lots of people don't like to eat broccoli. If you don't like to eat broccoli, then being a 1L will probably not change whether you will be eating it or not. As a reminder, there is no rule in law school that you must eat vegetables that you don't like. Answer D is wrong because nothing will ever validate taking political science as an undergraduate major. Answer B is wrong because the reason you are staying up all night as a 1L is not because you are staying up to party like it's 1999 (that's based on the Prince song, not that 1999 had particularly intense or enjoyable partying). Therefore, answer C is the correct answer. Don't have a conniption. Learning to speak *legalese* is a very good skill to have in a country that is inundated with legal documents. Even if you drop out of law school and run away to some remote island, knowing some *legalese* could help you negotiate the rights to your fascinating life story.

5. Sadly, you have been tricked again if you picked answer E. The title "None of the Above" would not make a good title for almost any chapter. While the

sentiments in answers B and D are true, neither would really capture the spirit of the chapter. Answer C is wrong because there are no buffalos in Chapter 5. Answer A is the correct answer because the title "One is the Loneliest Number" doesn't make as much sense as "Your Introduction to *Legalese*", unless you realize that being a 1L is lonely because you are studying all the time, are under stress all the time, and really have no time for simple human contact. Besides, when you do have human contact, it will start to take the form of constant competition or nitpicking or worse. So, indeed, being a first year law student can be a quite lonely experience. Stop crying now.

Chapter 5 Take-Aways

The first year of law school is a trying time. You start your journey from ordinary person to lawyer. You might be told that you are entering an elite club (the legal profession) but, unlike most clubs, the only benefit will be that you will work like crazy.

1. One is a lonely number and most likely the loneliest.

2. Legal memoranda, unlike regular memoranda, involve a lot of legal talk, we lawyers like to call *legalese*.

3. Blue Booking sucks.

4. Restatements of the law are marvelous distillations of judicial legal opinions. You should read them all.

6

Hiding the Law

As a first year student in law school, you will most likely have to take all the courses that are required by the curriculum: torts, contracts, a legal writing class, and probably constitutional law.

Different schools have different requirements.[16]

What is funny is that you thought you knew what you were getting yourself into when you applied to law school. In reality, there is nothing funny about it.

Law is not taught like other subjects.

Law school classes aren't taught like normal classes. In a normal class you get a textbook, the teacher tells you stuff, you write it down, and then you learn it. You take a test every so often and your life continues.

---

[16] Duh.

Law school is the exact opposite.

Your textbook isn't a textbook. It is a casebook. It has a series of cases. You will read these cases and say "huh?" to yourself or out loud.

The case holds some inner secret knowledge called the *rule*. You are supposed to read these cases and *spot the issues* and determine the *rule*. This method of constructing a course book came from the geniuses at Harvard.[17]

They thought that it would be a far superior method of learning than just having a book with the rules of law, so that you could memorize the damn thing and feed it back on an exam.

The so-called *case method* of teaching the law is so time-honored that by criticizing it here in this book I have committed a venial sin against the powers that be. It's no laughing matter because the law school establishment thinks the *case method* is the best. They don't take criticism well.

Naturally, humans can't learn the law with by the *case method*, so they need to go out and buy and all sorts of books that either discuss the cases in the casebooks and reveal the secret rule or simply list the rules and the reasons behind them.

I was lucky enough to have a professor who taught from these cheat books because it made much more sense. He had gotten tenure many years in the past, so he could do what he wanted.

He taught in way that humans could understand.

---

[17] That's a laugh.

Therefore, he was reviled by the faculty and loved by the students, far and away the favorite professor of most of the student body.

Socrates is turning over in his grave.

This brings me to the typical teaching method. It's called *hide the ball* because the typical professor spends most of the lesson trying to get us to reach the proper conclusion with all sorts of witty questions. That is the situation if you have a good professor. If you have a rotten and mean professor, then the professor will try to make you look like a fool, lead you down a wrong path, or just hide the rule as long as it's possible. Most law professors fall into this latter category. Called the *Socratic Method*, this teaching style has less to do with the philosopher Socrates and more to do with vicious mind games.

Be prepared to be humiliated standing up. When you are called on, you will most likely have to stand up. You will most likely have to recite the facts of the case. If you get any of the facts wrong, the professor is likely to make fun of you and move on to someone else.

Then it will be time to discuss the rule.

A word of caution. If you are using any of the cheat books (and there are only a limited number of them for each subject), be warned that the professors have read them, too, and that they know what they say. So if you quote them verbatim you will be found out.

Don't be found out.

The cheat books are not quite complete. They skip details.[18] Sometimes, they even get things wrong.

My advice would be to read the cheat book and then read the case in the casebook. I hear the howls already decrying the advice to read twice as much.

If you just read the casebook, you'll have no clue what's going on. Some of those cases from England in the 1600s can be a bit obscure.[19]

If you just read the cheat books, you'll have limited information and you will sound like you just read the cheat books when you open your mouth.

If the professor thinks you are just reading the cheat books, you will likely be made fun of, berated, ridiculed, and called on again and asked for specific points in the case which you won't know so you will be made fun of, berated and ridiculed even more. Rinse. Repeat.

This *hide the ball* teaching method can be so effective that by the middle of the semester, you won't even know where you are let alone where any ball is.

Also, by mid-semester you might think it's time for a test. Silly you. Why would you think that? Most law classes have only one test at the end of the semester. Usually there is no homework, no quizzes, and classroom participation may not count.

The fact that classroom participation doesn't count is because there are always a few people who need to make

---

[18] Naturally or else they would just be a reprint of the casebooks.

[19] Please note: *a bit* is extreme understatement.

their point and they usually make their point every class. And usually several times every class. Try as they might, the professors are virtually powerless to constantly avoid those eager students with the constantly raised hands. The worst offenders are your fellow classmates who have to prop their raised arm up with the other arm. Don't sit next to those people.

Playing musical chairs.

Unfortunately, your seat might not be of your choosing. You might be forced to sit alphabetically. The most likely scenario is that the seats you take on your first day are your seats for the remainder of the semester. If you have a nice professor, the seats you take in your second class in that course will be your seats for the semester. This way at least you have some idea whom you do and don't want to sit next to.

Another thing about first semester is that the classes are usually in rooms so large that you didn't think there were rooms that large. They were certainly not the rooms they showed you when you came to interview or for a tour. If you happened by those rooms on your tour, you were told that just some of your first classes will be in those rooms. While that statement might be the truth, it still means that you will spend most of your first year of law school in classrooms bigger than your parents' house.[20]

---

[20] And the bathrooms are outside (the room).

Nonetheless, you will soon determine in that group of 100 or more fellow students, who is the annoying one,[21] who is so shy that they will develop some twitch when called on, who is conservative, and who is liberal.[22]

As you read the cases and discover the rules, what you can determine about yourself is whether you are the type of person who loves rules or are the type of person who wants to get around the rules. As a renegade, you might like to find your way around the rules — it's more fun. Some people think it's even more fun to make the rules.[23]

My best advice is to be prepared. The first time I was called in law school was in a class on legal theory that was a required first year course. I had met the professor while walking to the orientation lunch the week before. Professors have the habit of calling on people in alphabetical order. So with my last name, I was destined to be called on late in the semester in most classes. This professor realized that. That's why I was the first student he called on in our first class.

He called on me and said, "since you won't be heard in the rest of your classes for quite some time, I will give the opportunity to be heard here and now."

I hadn't done the reading. I was about to be crucified.

The readings were various stories by Franz Kafka and

---

[21] You can bet there will be several.

[22] Fyi for all you grammar freaks, instead of using the more grammatical *he or she*, I am using the colloquial *they* (same goes with *him or her* and *his or hers* being replaced with *them* and *their*, respectively). I'm having fun creating my own grammar.

[23] Egomaniacs, please take note.

other writers of his ilk.

Miraculously, I had read Kafka in high school and especially remembered the story where a guy turns into an insect.[24]

For the next hour, it was the professor, Kafka, and me. I was able to answer every question and appeared to my classmates as the most prepared person they had ever met. At the end of class, many came up to me, introduced themselves, and asked me how I could have possibly have kept up with the professor's questions.

Since you might not have the opportunity to have read Kafka in high school, I suggest you read a few of his stories now.

Most law schools won't be discussing Kafka in any class, but it's better than scaring yourself to death by looking at a casebook before you go to law school.

---

[24] *The Metamorphosis* written by Franz Kafka in 1916.

Quiz concerning hiding the law

1. Why would Socrates be turning over in his grave?
   a. Because the ground he's buried in is very rocky and uncomfortable.
   b. To alert people that he may not be dead.
   c. Because of Harvard Law School.
   d. It's a Greek thing.
   e. Because he's using the Socratic Method underground.

2. Why is the law not taught the way everything else is taught?
   a. It's the law.
   b. Law schools like to think of themselves as being unique.
   c. Go figure!
   d. Self-appointed geniuses decided it would be better to make it more complex.
   e. All of the above reasons.

3. Where would be the worst place to sit in torts class?
   a. Next to the loudest talker.
   b. Next to the idiot with his hand raised for every question.
   c. Next to the idiot who never has the right answer.
   d. Near the exit.
   e. Down in front.

Quiz Answers

I was thinking of hiding the answers, in kind of homage to this chapter, but on second thought that would be inappropriate.

1. Saying that Socrates was turning over in his grave was simply a figure of speech. Therefore, Socrates would not be turning over in his grave for any reason associated with Socrates himself. In that sense, answers D and E are incorrect. Answer A is wrong because we don't know what kind of ground Socrates was buried in. Answer B could possibly be correct if somehow Socrates was still alive. However, it is doubtful that Socrates is still alive. Therefore, Harvard Law School gets the blame because they deserve it, making answer C the correct answer.

2. Answer E is the trick answer because not all the other answers are correct. There is no statute that requires the law to be taught in such a crazy way, so answer A is incorrect. Law schools don't have a personality, so answer B is incorrect. It is because of self-appointed geniuses that we have to learn the law using the case method, therefore, answer D is correct and answer C is wrong, because we have figured it out.

3. The worst place to sit in torts class is next to the person who never gets any question right because the professor will see you sitting right next to him and will instinctively call on you when that student next to you fails for the umpteenth time. Answer C is the correct response. The other responses are wrong because although all the other responses have their negatives they also have their positives. Sitting next to the loudest talker might mean that you never hear the professor. But that could be a good thing. Sitting next to a person who always has his arms raised for every question could be bad because it looks like you never know the answer unless you have your arm raised, too, but it might be good because you might never be called on. Sitting down in front is bad because you are away from the fun in the middle of the room but it is also good because it looks like you are enthusiastic for torts. Sitting near the exit makes you look like someone who wants to leave class in a hurry, which might not endear you to the professor, although it would allow you to sneak out of class if you had to. So, the correct answer is still C. It might be different if the class is contracts or constitutional law.

Chapter 6 Take-Aways

In law school, the professors will do their best to make you suffer. Supposedly they are doing it for your own good, but we know better. Here's what to remember when they tell you why they are hiding the law from you.

1. Socrates is blamed for a lot of things he has no control over because he's been dead a long time.

2. The "hide the ball" method of teaching the law is not done in most countries. Therefore, since the rest of the world is far less litigious than the United States, perhaps lawyers are suing so much over here because they are so pissed off at having to have learned the law in such a horrible way, and it is their payback to society.

3. Buy a lot of those cheat books but read the casebooks, too.

4. It's fun to make the rules, so play the game while you have to, then get out in the real world and make the rules anew.

No Horses in the Park

Or How the Rules Don't Make Much Sense

Returning to our story about legal memoranda in Chapter 5, we learned that legal memo writing is a fun exercise because at first it will seem that within every case there is some nugget of truth, some proposition of the law, some salient rule, that some judge set in stone.

There are books that break down the law into myriad subjects. Within those subjects there are sub-topics and so on until you get to particular rules.

Now the fun begins.

The Rule

The rule might be *no horses in the park*.

You find, through cross indexing a maze of books, or by looking it up on one of the legal databases that the university gets for free, that some case has the rule *no horses in the park*.

Just an aside, you are paying a lot for your law school education, so use those databases to your heart's content. When you are actually working in a law firm, it will cost the firm many thousands of dollars to use those legal databases, and then you're clients, not you, get to foot that bill. What a nice change.

Anyway, back to our hypothetical (made up story).

Case 1: the Pony

You find in the first case that the court dealt with someone who brought a pony into the park. The court ruled that the pony is not a horse because the legislature intended that only full-grown animals not be admitted to the park. Therefore, the pony can stay in the park.

How did the judge know the legislature's intent? The experienced lawyer knows the answer: the judge made it up. However, in the first semester of first year law school, you are taught that the judge consulted the Oracle at Delphi and also sacrificed a goat to determine the legislature's intent.

You must be impressed with the court's legal reasoning? No?

Give it time and you won't be impressed with any of it. At first, though, when you read those convoluted cases from 17th century England, you'll be amazed – amazed – to find any legal reasoning in them at all.

Even though you might not be impressed, you will need

to do more legal research.

Case 2: the Statue

You find another case where there was a statue of a horse erected in the center of the park and upon it was the likeness of the original owner of the land (after being stolen from the native Americans) one Fineas G. Davenport III. Somehow, someone sued and the case went up to an appellate court and some idiot judge ruled that the statue of the horse must be removed because of the *no horses in the park* rule.

The judge wrote that there couldn't be horses (full grown) in the park because of the rule. So they knock the statue down and have Fineas ride on a stone pony.

Case 3: the Zebra

Another case, more recent, involved a zebra in the park.

We all know that a zebra is not a horse.[25] Nonetheless, the genius on the bench in the zebra case determines that the zebra has to be removed form the park and barred from reentry because a zebra is enough like a horse that the statute applies to full grown zebras.

Regarding the last paragraph, lawyers are smiling and

---

[25] My 3-year old nephew knows that zebras aren't horses, too, but what might be common knowledge to a 3-year old is often unknown to the judiciary.

the non-lawyers are shaking their head in disbelief. Sorry you unbelievers. That's the way the law works.

You are a first year student and you have to write a legal memorandum. You are given a case involving a mule that has been used for years to pull the water wheel that powers the park's generator. You have to come to a conclusion as to whether the suit brought to the court to remove the mule will succeed or fail based on the law.

You might argue that if a zebra is out, then certainly a mule. But the mule might be small like a pony, so maybe the mule stays.

What about the Mule?

You have to examine the cases more carefully. Cases are categorized as to whether they affirm a previous ruling, are distinguished from the previous ruling, or are overturned.

Note that when I say *distinguished*, it is not in the sense of "my distinguished colleague will now tell us the mystery of life" but rather *distinguished* in the sense of whether you can distinguish between a jalapeño and even hotter peppers. Many legal cases have the same effect as eating too many peppers.

Forget about all that case analysis here, because if I make the example too complex you'll put this book on your dresser and forget to finish it and then I will see it a few years from now on someone's table at a garage sale and they'll say, "oh, it's okay, but I never finished it" and I will go home and sulk a bit and have to watch a Bill Murray comedy just to get that smile on my face and spring in my step.

So, does the mule make it into the park? By this time, you couldn't care, but you have to write the damn memo anyway.

Write that legal memo!

You might wrack your brains out trying to determine the right answer. You might even write something and think it's so totally off base that you pound the damn memo into your bed for an hour and then go to see if a friend of yours who is studying in the library will talk you into staying in law school, which they probably will.

An enemy might also talk you into staying in law school, thinking that the totally stressed out student will lower the grade curve. Yes, that's how lovely some people are in law school. These are the same people who rip out necessary cases from the casebooks in the law library. They also make partner at some of the nasty law firms.

The point of your writing your first legal memorandum in law school is not to show you how to convey the meaning of a nonsensical statute, nor to try to figure out what the judges were eating prior to writing their opinions since it had to be something that gave them upset stomachs because how could that idiot judge remove the stone horse.

If you actually read the case, you will find that Fineas actually hated horses and in the deed of his land to the county he specified that he didn't want any horses in the park. The mule working in the park was doing the same thing that Fineas's own mule used to do, so it seems that mules were okay. Now, whoever thought that Fineas would like to be on a statue of a horse needs to research Fineas's life a little better. The judge who let the pony in, though, obviously didn't know what the intent was.

What's the point?

The point for the law student isn't that they get it correct, but rather that they suffer the torment of actually coming to some kind of conclusion based on all the nonsense.

Now you can see that the stress-induced memo-punching discussed in chapter 5 is actually the point of writing the first memorandum. What fun!

As you will find on the bar exam, any kind of conclusion is alright, as long as it is "well reasoned". What *well reasoned* means is usually how it's interpreted based on the politics of the reader, because judges have a habit of overlooking the facts.

To law professors, *facts* merely get in the way of ideology. So, you can see, that the whole legal system is a crock.

So, what happens to the poor mule? Does it get to stay in the park or is it exported to some country where mules are sacrificed to please the gods.

No one knows.

Why?

Because I made it all up.

Quiz concerning how the rules make no sense

1. Write a legal memorandum, examining all the case law, to determine if a mule can be brought into a park, where the town's statutes clearly state that no horses are allowed in the park.

2. Write an essay answering the question why you would make a good lawyer.

3. The way a judge rules on a case depends on which of the following:
    a. What the judge had for breakfast in the morning on the day he makes his decision.
    b. Which side offered the larger bribe.
    c. The law.
    d. The ghosts of long dead legislators convening in a séance to guide the judge to their intent.
    e. Whimsy.

Quiz Answers

You got so used to the insipid multiple choice questions that you never suspected that you would get essay-type questions.

1. How can you write a legal memorandum on this question when I specifically told you that I made the whole thing up? If you actually wrote a legal memo on this question then deduct a lotta points from you overall score. I don't know, like a 300 points. That should make you feel foolish. If you didn't write a legal memoranda, then deduct 150 points from your score (if you have been keeping score) because you can't follow directions. If you began to write a legal memorandum and then either gave up, cursed a lot, or punched something, give yourself 300 points plus experience points (whatever they are) for experiencing what all first year law students experience: frustration.

2. Are you kidding? I was. If you really, seriously, wrote an essay, I won't question your mental state. Nonetheless, you should have included points such as (1) is there really such a thing as a good lawyer, (2) you are argumentative and hope to alienate all your friends, and (3) that you even take humor books seriously.

3. How could you even think that judges take bribes? B is wrong. And judging is serious business; there is no whimsy in the law. A lot of arbitrariness, but no whimsy. So, answer E is wrong. Judges are imbued with the knowledge of legislative intent not from ghosts, but by making it up as they go along. Thus, answer D is wrong. Answer C is the trick response. The law says a lot of things, but none of it definitive, especially amongst lawyers. The correct answer is A, breakfast. As we know from other studies, breakfast is the most important meal of the day. And now that eggs are alright again (first they were great, then they had too much cholesterol, then they didn't have too much cholesterol, and now they are back to being great again – almost sounds like lawyers made this up instead of doctors), you can make sure that your judge gets enough protein. Also, raisin bran is a tasty treat. As of the date of publication, it has not been determined whether protein or fiber or other dietary ingredients predispose a judge to rule for the plaintiff or defendant. You're taking your chances when you offer your judge a blueberry muffin. Therefore, remember, don't feed the judges.

Chapter 7 Take-Aways

You probably thought that the rules are the rules. This brief chapter hopefully dispelled that mythical idea from your head.

1. The rules are arbitrary.

2. No one cares what is right. No one cares what you really think. As a lawyer, you are a hired gun, and you will argue the law the way your client wants it argued. If they want horses in the park, then you damn well better find case law that supports that argument. If they don't want horses in the park, then find case law that says that. Either way, you lose.

3. And just in case you think you might be going crazy, mules and zebras are not horses, while ponies are, or at least will be, horses.

The Mint Milano Diet

Or how I ate nothing but cookies the first semester
of first year law school and lost 20 pounds

You are writing memos and making all sorts of legal
stuff up in your brain. You finally realize that *no
horses in the park* means whatever the judge
thought it meant or wanted it to mean the morning he wrote
his decision.

Since a lot of different judges wrote a lot of different
things about what *no horses in the park* means, obviously
there has to be some non-uniform input into those judges.

That input is breakfast.

Some judges eat ham and eggs for breakfast while other
judges eat a whole grain cereal that looks great on the box
and in the TV commercials but tastes like cardboard in real
life.

These different breakfasts are what determine the variations in the law.

You think I'm making that up?

Diet not only affects your cardiovascular health but also whether or not your cousin Ernie will be able to get away with embezzling the assets of the computer firm he works for. Which brings me to the point of diet while in your first year of law school.

You might think that in law school you will be sitting[26] and learning all the time, so what goes in your mouth is not that important given what comes out.

Wrong.

All the crap you eat is just as important as the crap you spit out in class when the professor calls on you. Therefore, you have to have a diet that sustains you for all those tense moments.

Some people might turn to junk food and eat way too much because they are mimicking depression. Sad to say, but those people are actually depressed, they're not mimicking anything. They will eat and eat and eat until they are so crazed from high fructose corn syrup that they think that the *no horses in the park* rule means that Crazy Aunt Sadie's chicken can't go into the park. The statute is silent as to chickens.[27]

On the other side of the dieting extreme is your ex-girlfriend the vegetarian, who would become a vegan if she

---

[26] That's *sitting*; there's no *h* after the *s*.

[27] The *statute is silent* is *legalese* for *no one cares*.

attended law school. She will also be watching way too many movies on the Lifetime cable channel but that gets us into areas that this book is not going to deal with. And no, I'm not thinking of anyone in particular, I'm just making this up.

The main problem with law school is that you will be sitting and reading and you might neglect things like exercise or even walking. Therefore, there is the potential for you to gain millions of pounds (that's you collectively).

What I am suggesting as a remedy for that sedentary lifestyle is a diet so revolutionary, so fantastic, that it really should be the subject of an entire book and directed to an audience that really needs another pointless diet plan.

My diet is the Mint Milano diet. Below is a cross-sectional view of the cookie with its distinctive mint and chocolate layers.

Cross-section of Mint Milano

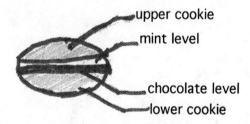

Posh tosh, you say?[28]

---

[28] Don't say *posh tosh*. There's always someone who will beat you up for saying *posh tosh*.

Au contraire![29]

If you want to lose all the weight you will gain from sitting around all day and night reading law books, then this diet will help you shed those pounds. Besides its obvious health benefits, it is delicious.

Therefore, you can choose this diet as a healthy and nutritious one, guaranteed to give you the vim and vigor you deserve.

<u>WARNING:</u>

There is <u>no guarantee</u> — the term _guarantee_, as used in this chapter, is only a figure of speech, which in this context expressly means there is _no guarantee_.

To calculate the amount of vim you deserve, take the number of pages you actually read in your legal textbook, divide that number by the number of pages in the cheat books (the ones that give you synopses of the cases and tell you the rules of law). If the result is greater than 1 then you deserve some vim. The vigor determination is obviously a much more complex equation. See your doctor or pharmacist for calculating your deserved vigor.

---

[29] Excellent use of French, n'est ce pas?

So what is the Mint Milano diet?

Simply put it is the diet of eating nothing but Mint Milanos.[30]

Stage direction:	Have one of those paid TV ad audiences in your head and have it be aghast at that statement (aghast in a good way). *Note: auditory delusions will help you better understand this diet.*

Have I intrigued you? Not yet?!

Pay attention. You don't want eat so much that Wal-Mart doesn't have clothes in your size and you don't want to go to the other extreme and eat sprouts at every meal.

This is a very simple diet; even a college student can do it.

First, though, you have to be committed (not to a mental institution, although that would help, but committed in the sense of being dedicated).

To begin this diet, you must buy two bags of Mint Milanos every day.

---

[30] Mint Milanos are a registered trademark of Pepperidge Farm and a really delicious cookie.

Mint Milanos are a delicious snack treat that consists of the interesting combination of mint and chocolate surrounded by a tasty cookie. Mmmm. You can just imagine the goodness. If you are having a hard time imagining the goodness, I suggest you go get some Mint Milanos. Don't wait until they go on sale for 50 cents cheaper, but do wait until you finish this chapter.

Don't try this diet with double chocolate Milanos. Don't try this diet with any other cookie in the Milano family nor even with my personal favorite, the delicious coconut flavored Tahiti cookies, (pictured to the right). You want Mint Milanos.  Even Orange Milanos won't work. For reasons only known to scientists, just the unique combination of mint, chocolate, and cookies yield the desired weight loss results.

And if you are thinking of doing this with Oreo cookies or Vienna Fingers, just forget it. All these other cookies have been tested under scientific conditions and it's really hard to lose 20 pounds eating them. Besides, they come in bigger bags and that might exceed the cookie-limit. It would be great if chocolate cupcakes with dark chocolate fudge icing were also diet foods, but sadly  they are not. These non-diet foods are pictured above.

Now, back to explaining the new diet that will guarantee you fantastic weight loss.

By the way, there is <u>no guarantee</u>!

Take the two bags of Milanos and separate them.[31]

Take one with you as you run out the door to your first class and don't eat them till lunch.

Once lunchtime comes around, you will get stares from people. I mean stares because of the cookies, not the stares that you are usually getting from others for reasons that are unique to you. And I'm sure they have no reason to stare, but people are rude. Nonetheless, now they will stare because of your bag of cookies (don't make any innuendo here).

Someone obnoxious but loveable will ask in an incredulous tone, "is that all you're eating for lunch."

You can answer yes. But don't share!

---

[31] We'll save the discussion of how multiple bags of cookies placed too close can form a critical mass.

No sharing because we need the diet to work and sharing at this point in the diet will deprive you of the nourishment you need.

If someone has the gall to ask you for a cookie, tell them you are on the Mint Milano diet.

If they snicker and laugh, explain it to them, but in a condescending way that makes them feel foolish.

If they have a knowing but still curious look on their face, buy them a copy of my book and hand it to them in a way that conveys that they should have read my book before they went to law school and while it is probably too late for them to get any benefit out of it they should be warned anyway of what life has in store for them and you care enough to tell them.

Or, you could just nod.

If they look at you how a mother looks at her child as it eats grass in the backyard and then vomits all over the newly cleaned kitchen floor, then tell them you have to read the book in front of you for the next class. And say it in a dismissive tone so they know who's getting the honors grade in that class. That person would be you, not them.

Once you eat the entire bag of Mint Milanos, you will be feeling on top of the world because of the delightful flavor combination. Ahhhhh.

Or, you might be feeling sick to your stomach because even too much of a good thing can be bad. But don't think that. Let's keep the illusion going that I actually have something interesting to say.

The real secret of the Mint Milano diet is how, with bag 2, we turn that lovely favor combination into your worst nightmare.

Get bag 2.

You can start eating the second bag of Milanos around dinnertime.

I advise you to eat the bag in a public place because by the middle of bag 2 you will be wondering what the hell you are doing eating two bags of Mint Milanos.

By the time you eat cookie 6 of bag 2, the mint/chocolate/cookie combination will start to make you ill.

Cookie 7, even a bit worse.

By cookie 8 you'll wonder why you didn't share your earlier bag of cookies with your friends.

The reason that you didn't share the first bag is that for the diet to work you have to get to the point where you are eating so many of these cookies that you start to feel sick.

Naturally, even though I appear to be suggesting it, I'm not really advocating that anyone eat so many cookies as to make themselves sick.

At cookie 9 you will think that maybe it would be a good idea to get some real food. Even a baloney sandwich will seem appetizing now. And I don't mean the delicious gourmet baloney that you are accustomed to but rather the really crappy baloney that you can only buy in packages (and the baloney is really thick) — that's the baloney that you will be thinking of.

At cookie 10, you will realize that you can't finish the second bag of cookies and you also realize that you have now eaten too much to actually eat real food. The thought of real food will start to turn you off unless there is someone eating one of those instant chicken noodle soups near you.

Eat the cookies in the library lounge, which normally doesn't allow food to be eaten there, but they let you get away with eating the cookies as long as you don't make crumbs.

At cookie 11 you were hoping that there wasn't another level of cookies in the bag (the bags are scientifically divided into three tiers of cookies in a lovely paper pouch, each layer pouch holding 5 cookies) and that cookie ten was really the end of the bag. However, cookie 10 is not the end, you have five more cookies to go. Five more.

You have eaten twenty-five high fat cookies and you have five more left.

You can do it — tell yourself that.

Ignore your homunculus.[32]

---

[32] Your homunculus is the little person that lives in your head — I told you auditory hallucinations would help.

It will try to convince you that you can't do it.

But this is where the diet really works!

The mint/chocolate/cookie combination is now becoming repulsive. By cookie 12, you can't imagine how anyone could think that mint, chocolate, and cookie put together is a good idea.

At cookie 13, someone who you want to impress comes by and sees you really thinking hard about something. That person will think that you are thinking about what a *tort* is and that you have the answer in your brain.

What you are really thinking about is the 13th cookie of your second bag of Mint Milanos and wondering why the hell you started eating these things in the first place.

The person asks you what you are doing. We'll call her Leeloo.[33]

You do *not* reply that you are on the Mint Milano diet and that you feel sick. As we noted earlier, Mint Milanos are fantastic cookies. It's just that eating two bags of them will prove that too much of a good thing can be repulsive.

---

[33] We'll use Leeloo here for lack of a better name if you are an unmarried male looking for female companionship. By the way, if you haven't seen Milla Jojovich with Bruce Willis in the hit movie *The Fifth Element* (the ultimate edition is available on dvd right now, so put it in your wishlist if you don't decide to drop this book and go out and purchase it right now), Leeloo is quite attractive. You can also come up with your own fantasy name depending on whom you wish to fantasize about. Maybe I'm just thinking fondly of someone else and just using the name Leeloo instead of her real name, which might be close. It's all fictitious.

Instead, you say, "I think I got it — what I was reading makes sense. Hey, you want a cookie." Please be as subtle as possible.

Can you give away cookie 13?

Yes if you haven't handled it too much. Give away cookie 14 if you have handled cookie 13 too much.

No sane person will refuse the offer of a Mint Milano. They might hesitate, but if they do, then you nudge a little.

No one, not even the beautiful Leeloo, who might be excessively watching her weight, can refuse the tasty and tempting Mint Milano.

On second thought, give Leeloo cookie 14, as you know you've handled cookie 13 too much and it just wouldn't look right to give her cookie 13. Then you can eat cookie 13 while she eats cookie 14 and bond of some spiritual yet also rawly sexual level. Remember that you actually have to prepare for class, so this wouldn't be a good time to live your fantasy or even to fantasize. Let her enjoy the cookie. Don't stare.

The final cookie, cookie 15 of bag 2, still sits in the bag.

You will probably sit the bag down on your library table in disgust. People will walk by and nod in your direction. In this nod there is a silent announcement that you have the good taste and refinement to eat one of the world's best cookies. This announcement might not reach you (no, not just because it is a silent announcement) because you are so sick of eating nothing but cookies all day that the thought of that last cookie just sitting there in that bag — you can hear it mocking you. The cookie says *eat me, eat me, I'm delicious, you can't resist.*

The person walking by giving you this silent announcement doesn't seem to hear the cookie. Meanwhile, the cookie taunts you in ever-louder pleas to be eaten. The only recourse is to get up, grab the cookie bag and catch up to the silent announcer and offer them the cookie.

Naturally, they will retort, once they look in the bag and see only one cookie, saying *but that is your last cookie; I can't eat your last cookie; that is a very kind offer, but being that it is your very last cookie, I wouldn't dream of eating it!*

At this point don't blurt out, *please take the damn cookie because I'm so sick of eating nothing but cookies!*

This plea for help will only make you look like a complete loser, an idiot, and someone more than slightly off kilter.

Such a response will also have the intended recipient take a few steps back from you and look at you in the same way that people in all Biblical movies look at the lepers.[34]

No, no. Bad form. You want to have that person take a cookie from you and not pull out their cell phone to dial 911, nodding nervously while looking at you with a weird smile.

It would be far better for you to say that you've eaten most of the bag yourself and that you would be far happier if

---

[34] Except for Charlton Heston in *Ben Hur* who hugged his poor leprosy-afflicted mother and ran into the leper cave to retrieve his sister (naturally with the help of the man whose tongue was cut out — or am I not remembering the movie accurately — perhaps I've had too much sugar.)

they ate the cookie. Don't have a strange grin on your face as you make your cookie suggestion, though, or again the intended recipient will slowly reach for their cell phone, while nodding and grinning at you.

Better still, approach Leeloo, who is sitting in another table a little further away and place the cookie on her stack of books. She's already accepted one cookie from you and so whatever diet she was on is totally ruined. Thus, another cookie won't make a bit of difference. As she looks up, trying to dissuade you from leaving the cookie there, you can smile at her with a confident, romantic smile, open your eyes a little wider, and then walk away.

She may insist that you take it back. If it's not a phony excuse because she would truly want to have another delicious Mint Milano cookie, then you can tell her that she is free to donate the cookie to whomever she wishes. Then you can smile at her with a confident romantic smile, open your eyes little wider, and then walk away.

If there's no Leeloo in the room (and please remember folks, that Leeloo is my fantasy girl; you can choose you own combination of cookie-giver and romantic interest and make up your own names) and no silent announcer, you can do one of two things.

First, you can force the cookie on someone. You can actually stick the cookie in someone's mouth. On second thought, don't stick a cookie in someone else's mouth. Such action could open you up to all sorts of legal liability, which you'll learn all about in torts class.

Second, you can eat the cookie yourself. You might eat

the cookie quickly. You might eat the cookie slowly. But as you eat the cookie, you will know that you have eaten way, way, way too many cookies.

You can look forward to day 2, when you get to consume another two bags of cookies.

By week 3, you will probably be donating more and more cookies.

If you donate all the cookies in the bag 2, you're off the diet.

Why?

Because if you donated all of bag 2, you might still be hungry and so you might get some real food for yourself.

Just keep feeding yourself the cookies.

After you have been on the Mint Milano Diet for several weeks, you can say that you live on them because after several weeks on the Mint Milano diet, you will be so sick of mint, chocolate and cookie inhabiting your part of the universe that you will lose 20 pounds.

I lost 20 pounds my first semester of law school and I am sure it is because of the Mint Milano diet.

OR

Losing 20 pounds first semester of first year law school might have been caused by the stress of starting law school, in which case it means that you can ignore all this cookie diet nonsense.

By the way, don't throw out cookie fifteen from bag two. Eat it up.

Enjoy.

It's not that I'm evil; I'm just a renegade.

A reminder of
The Mint Milano Diet
disclaimer.

I'm not really suggesting that you eat nothing but cookies and lose weight in the process. It's a joke. Get over it.

That much being said, I really did eat an awful lot of cookies and really did lose 20 pounds. However, it's probably not a good idea. So don't do the Mint Milano Diet. Enjoy Milanos; don't abuse them. Also, for those legally minded readers, I did not receive any endorsement from Pepperidge Farm nor have they expressed any opinion on their cookie's remarkable weightloss properties.

Actually, the weightloss was probably just due to the stress of the first semester. But eating cookies all the time can't hurt, can it?

That was a rhetorical question, which means you don't have to answer it. If you actually want to answer questions, then leave Socrates in his grave and simply go to the next page and take the end-of-chapter quiz.

Quiz concerning the Mint Milano Diet

1. Sorry folks, we're starting off with the reading comprehension question. Why were there "on second thought" statements made in the reading?

    a. The author assumes that because the law is based on the adversary system, that there will always be someone second-guessing your actions and you should start thinking like the opposition.

    b. No reason. On second thought, maybe there was a very good reason.

    c. Eating nothing but cookies all day, no matter what brand or type, will reduce your brain to second-guessing.

    d. Don't second-guess. On the LSAT, as with any other standardized test, go with your gut response. In real life, though, when giving cookies to other people, it is a good idea to give them a clean and fresh cookie. So if your first thought was to give them the cookie that you have been mauling, it would be better to give it a second thought and give them a nice, clean cookie instead.

    e. The chapter was written like one of those stream of consciousness poems you read in high school, which made no sense then and don't make any now.

2. What is more earth-shattering, the Mint Milano Diet or the point in the movie *Dante's Peak* when Pierce Brosnan's character tells the town not to panic just a second before the roof caves in?

    a. The Mint Milano Diet because it defies all the conventional wisdom.

    b. The scene in *Dante's Peak* because of the irony.

    c. Neither the diet nor the movie because the diet is a farce and the movie, while having some riveting scenes and being well-acted, is a work of fiction.

    d. There were no lawyers in *Dante's Peak*, so why is it even brought up here. It wasn't even in the stupid chapter. These questions are getting totally pointless, almost like the third year of law school.

    e. Perhaps a diet based on the Tahiti cookie and eaten while in Tahiti, at one of those fancy resorts, like in that Harrison Ford movie *Six Days, Seven Nights* (which my brother didn't like – yes, the brother with the computer program).

3. Please calculate the number of cookies you would need to consume if you wanted to lose 25 pounds.

    a. That is an unfair question because I was guaranteed that there would be no math in law school.

b. You would have to buy a third bag of cookies, share 12 of them, and eat the rest.

c. Forget it, you'll never lose 25 pounds.

d. Eating cookies to lose weight! What, are you crazy?!

e. The diet has been denied on appeal.

4. Examine the pie chart below and together with your knowledge gathered from this chapter, determine which statement is the most correct (i.e., the correctest).

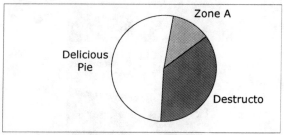

a. You can't use a pie chart to describe cookies. Duh!

b. Zone A is the zone a person would be in when they are in "the zone".

c. Destructo is evil.

d. The rest of the pie should be eaten for maximum weight loss.

e. I can't determine a damn thing.

5. Which picture below depicts the amount of cookies you should have eaten before you share any?

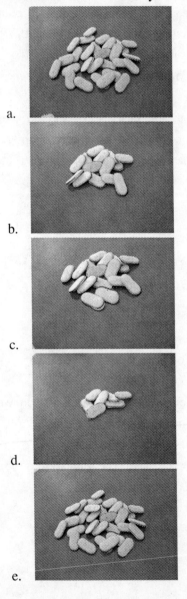

a.

b.

c.

d.

e.

6. The Cookie Monster is to a supermodel as a law student on the Mint Milano Diet is to
   a. an idiot.
   b. a supermodel.
   c. Ernie and Bert.
   d. a medical student.
   e. a bulimic.

7. Can other cookies be substituted for Mint Milanos?
   a. Yes, Amaretto Milanos, but you have to eat 4 full bags and you can't share any until two months into the program.
   b. Yes, any cookie will work because the diet is magic.
   c. Yes, because eating cookies makes people lose weight, no matter what cookies are eaten.
   d. No, because I read the chapter.
   e. No, because the whole idea is idiotic.

Quiz Answers

There were a lot of questions in this chapter because diet is such an important topic. Let's see how you stack up against these questions.

1. The correct answer was B. On second thought, maybe one of the other responses was the best answer. On third thought, skip this question, as there are too many questions at the end of this chapter. If you spent a lot of time thinking about the answer to question 1, then you should ask yourself, why are you spending a lot of time on trying to answer questions in a humor book.

2. The correct answer is A because no one ever expected the Mint Milano Diet. Answer B is wrong, because you instinctively know that the roof will cave in. The other responses have their good points but don't really answer the question. On second thought, a trip to Tahiti wouldn't be a bad way to lose weight.

3. For answer C to be correct, you would have to look deeply into your own heart and answer honestly. Answer A is the most correct answer, because if you knew how to do math, you'd be applying to medical school.

4. I am sure that you can deduce something, so answer E is incorrect. Answers B, C, and D are just testing your resolve. Answer A is the correct answer because it's just so obvious that a pie chart can't be used for cookies.

5. The correct answer is A. Count them yourself.

6. We're looking for opposites here. Answers B and E are the same thing, and neither is correct. A is the angry person's answer. C is the goofy person's answer. The correct person's answer is D, medical student, because the opposite of a law student is a medical student. At least that is what professors in law school will say. Medical school professors will just tell you to avoid lawyers.

7. Seven questions for this chapter – that's a lot. Perhaps we'll consider this a bonus question, because don't forget that we threw out question 1 on a technicality (I'm not quite sure what was so technical about it, but what the hell). Answers A and C are wrong and were only put there to weed out people who thought they would get into an accredited law school. They won't if they answered A or C. Answer B is for the Harry Potter crowd, but it's also wrong because the only magic in this book is the look in Leeloo's eyes when you tell her you love her. Um, wait a minute. Forget that last part.

There is no magic. Damn. So, the correct answer is either D or E. Unfortunately, while E is true, the best answer is D because this question is given every year and that's the answer we're sticking, too. Besides, this is a bonus question, so don't sweat it.

Chapter 8 Take-Aways

Making up something as silly as a cookie diet is very similar to what you will face in court when your really guilty client wants you to come up with some off-the-wall idea to get him acquitted. Ah, maybe there was some point to this chapter after all.

1. There was no point to this chapter.

2. You can lose weight doing a lot of crazy things, even eating nothing but cookies, but it might be better to eat a well-balanced meal for dinner after eating a whole bunch of crap the rest of the day.

3. When making up silly arguments (such as advocating a cookie diet to lose weight) in court, make sure that you back them up with case law citations, that you use expert testimony (that you will have to pay a bundle for), and that you keep a straight face (because giggling through your argument could make it appear weak). And don't forget to eat your vegetables.

9

Legal Overload

After a few days, weeks, or months of law school, you might find yourself at home one evening in front of the television set flicking the remote control from one channel to the next. At first this might seem like a good thing to you. You're not studying; you're doing something you like. Right?

Wrong. It might seem that you are surfing the spectrum in order to finding something to watch, something to enjoy. However, after a half-hour of going from one channel to the next, you will sense a certain amount of aimlessness.

Are you in search of a show on TV that doesn't exist? Are you desperately missing reading another stupid case for Torts class? No, neither of those lovely alternatives.

The diagnosis is that you are burned-out.

You might have experienced aimless channel surfing in the past. But this is not your run-of-the-mill channel surfing. You are not looking for something you would like to watch.

Indeed, you might flick past something that you would normally like to watch. If you have the presence of mind to realize that you just surfed by a show you would have liked to have watched, then you might begin to comprehend the state that you are in.

And whether that state is California or some rustbelt state, your state of mind will be even more important. You are in dire straits if you are burned out.

Burnout will prevent you from concentrating and getting work done, which could be a problem.

When law school starts to overwhelm you, you might be too busy to recognize that you are being overwhelmed. It might even take a few days of channel surfing before you understand that you have a problem.[35]

In the meantime, while you have been aimlessly surfing, your work has been piling up. You have been so busy sitting and doing nothing that you can't get anything done. If things are piling up that badly, then you are at *critical stage burnout*.

Burnout is no laughing matter. And neither is this chapter. I figure since I spent all that time in the last chapter on that ludicrous cookie diet, the least I could do for you here is to take a serious look at how law school causes

---

[35] Isn't it good to know that the television can now be used as a diagnostic tool?

burnout and what you can do to overcome it.

Eating a lot of cookies might seem like a cure, but stick with this chapter for a bit more concrete solutions, such as movie therapy.

If you are experiencing the symptoms of burnout, then the more you continue to do nothing to cure your burnout the deeper your depression will become. You might even take to punching your first legal memorandum into your mattress.

You might do what a lot of people do their first semester of law school, namely, wonder how the hell they could have thought that they would like to be a lawyer.

Dropping out of law school is not the best method for overcoming burnout.

Did you really think you would like to be a lawyer? Reviewing in your mind what we discussed earlier in this book (don't review it too much or you'll get a nose bleed), the practice of law does seem to be portrayed in the media as a powerful, fun profession. However, as I have mentioned, there is some stress when attending law school and working as a lawyer.

A lot of people drop out of law school their first semester. They drop out not because they aren't smart enough but because the stress got to them in such a poignant way that they didn't know what else to do.

Or, they just came to their senses.

But let's concentrate on overcoming burnout and staying

in law school. The best thing to do is to recognize that law school will get you down. Therefore, it might be helpful if I revealed the cure.

The cure to late stage burnout might be a trip to Cancun, Mexico, but that might interfere with your classes.

Go to Cancun.

Like diverting an incoming, earth-bound asteroid, it is easier to take action sooner rather than later. Better to nip it in the bud before it becomes full-blown burnout. See the movie *Armageddon*, if you need to continue this analogy. Anyway, at the early stage the cure is simpler.

As soon as you notice that you are sitting in front of the TV aimlessly changing channels, stop and go do something fun.

Yes, fun.

Fun does not mean reading cases in your Constitutional Law textbook. Fun does not mean turning off the TV and worrying. Fun does not mean sitting in the law library and reading some cases from the 1800s.

Fun is not legal issue.

Fun means taking a few days off from law school.

Since there are no tests and virtually no collected homework assignments during the semester, the worst that can happen to you is that you are made a fool of in class. That fate is better than the alternative of drifting ever more deeply into burnout. Besides, you will be made a fool of in class anyway.

Long-term burnout is really depressing because it's just like depression and getting out of that funk is hard work. So take the easy way out. Go to the beach; go on a hike; go get a banana split. There is no need to get falling-down drunk but have some fun.

Doing something fun will
help defeat burnout.

By the way, when I say do something fun, I don't mean organizing a game of Monopoly with your fellow classmates. That wouldn't be fun. It would be annoying.

No matter how fun your law school friends are (we're using the term *friends* quite loosely here), they are still some of the most highly competitive people in the country. Playing a board game with them will just enhance that competition. It certainly won't relieve stress unless you win so big that you can humiliate all the others. However, you might not want to humiliate your friends. More importantly, you might not win.

Take a long walk or a long drive.

Flirt with someone but don't try to pick them up. You don't need the pressure. Remember, you're burned out and trying to cure yourself. Ignore this suggestion, just get that banana split – it's healthy and great tasting.

Buy yourself something that you always wanted but always denied yourself. Unless it will cause you further grief, because it's too expensive or it requires you to read it or build it or otherwise stress over it. Forget it – have the banana split.

We're talking about engaging in some nonstressful activity. I know it's hard to think of something that won't give you stress while you're attending law school, but do it. Otherwise you will be sitting and channel surfing and stressing even more because even more of your work isn't getting done.

Talking yourself out of burnout won't work either.

Accept the fact that you won't accomplish something for the next couple of days.

Go see a movie (not a film) where things blow up (movie for men) or the romance works (movie for women).

If someone else is experiencing burnout, you might want to help them.[36] In fact, it might help both of you.[37]

Helping other people defeat their burnout is optional.

When you see a supposedly smart classmate underperforming, you might suggest that they take a little break.

If your school is hypercompetitive and your fellow classmate is inclined not to trust you, that might push them

---

[36] Note that I said *might*.

[37] *Ibid*. (*Ibid* means look at the last footnote because it applies here, too.)

over the edge. They could think that you are trying to take them away from the work that they already aren't doing.

Instead of creating that atmosphere, you can offer to go to a movie with them.

Or, you can say nothing and just watch them crash or burn.

But, in the best-case scenario, intervening might just be the decent thing to do.

Getting back to your own burnout crisis, at this point we can discuss my 3 stages of movies to get yourself out of a depression.

The 3 Stages of Movie Cures for Burnout

Stage 1: The Comedy

For the lightly depressed and those on the verge of burnout, Stage 1 is watching a goofy comedy. Something that makes you laugh because it's silly. An old Steve Martin movie or practically any Bill Murray movie will be applicable here.

Stage 2: The Mystery Movie

Stage 2 is mid-level depressed. A bit more depressed than you normally get when something doesn't work out for you. This stage is like breaking up with your short-term love interest (getting dumped is better because it's out of your control; for that, go back to Stage 1) or getting a seriously bad grade on a paper. What paper? Your first legal memorandum. The professor didn't like the crinkles from all the pounding. It certainly wasn't your writing. Certainly not.

You need to get your mind off of whatever it is that is upsetting you.

An engaging movie is the one to look for in Stage 2. Some kind of murder mystery is best. One that you haven't seen before so your mind actually works on the problem.

Get a classic Hitchcock film or some spy movie from the Cold War era. Remember, bad guys are the Nazis and the Soviets and people who act suspiciously.

You might also want to try some science fiction that has some unknown quantity and is a good movie. Not some really stupid *drilling to the center of the Earth* movie or something where a scientist turns people into disgusting creatures because he knows that all the misery he is creating will either make him rich, become ruler the world, or benefit mankind in some twisted way. Get a good movie instead.

Just see something that will engage your mind and something you haven't seen before.

Stage 3: The Musical or the Stooges

Stage 3 is when your long-term love interest breaks up, when you really bomb a class or paper, or when something even worse happens. *Something worse* could be that you find out after three months of law school that you still don't know what a tort is.

You need a movie so frivolous or ridiculous but still

entertaining that your mind can't help but be engaged and you can't help but smile. This runs the gamut anywhere from a Fred Astair musical to the Three Stooges.

The trick here is nothing heavy. Again, it's best that it's something you haven't seen before, even though you can presume that Fred will be dancing for no good reason or that the Stooges will get into some mishap where Moe will get angry.

If you had a real tragedy, my movie watching strategy might not be the best way to go. Perhaps talking to a loved one or seeking professional help would be in order. Yes, this is me showing actual concern. Touching, isn't it?

But for the typical ups and down of law school, movie therapy helps.

**The cure to burnout,
typified by aimlessly surfing TV channels,
is to go out and rent a movie.**

There could be other alternatives to movie therapy.

Perhaps you have someone to have consensual sex with. Naturally there are performance issues when under too much stress. So, sex might not be the best alternative.

Committing yourself to a mental institution could be an option, but the heavy drugs and the jacket with the arms tied around your back might interfere with your plans to complete the semester at school.

Prayer might work, but then again God might not be in favor of having more lawyers on Earth.

Having a room full of Lego might be helpful for some, but you really don't want your classmates dropping by while you are building a dinosaur out of Lego. They might hear you screaming that you don't have enough green bricks. Your embarrassment might not even be apparent to you. Your so-called friends in the parking area could hear you screaming about your lack of green Lego and turn around and leave without ever dropping in on you. They'll all be convinced that you've left sanity behind, which definitely is not good for getting potential study partners.[38]

So forget thinking up further alternatives and go get that movie.

When someone asks why you can't help with some paper, you tell them that there is this Fred Astair musical from the 1940s that you are dying to see because you are in a Stage 3 Movie Depression. They'll understand, I'm sure.

To sum it all up, depression is bad, but not doing something about it can be far worse.

Depression beyond movie therapy

If you get to the point where you think it was pointless to go to law school, you can do one of two things.

First, you can quit law school. That will end the stress of law school right away.

Naturally that will create a whole new bunch of stresses that you will have to deal with, like explaining why you left

---

[38] No, not based on actual events.

law school to future employers who won't take kindly to the fact that you couldn't handle the stress.

You better make up a really good reason that won't sound like total bullshit and also won't have you laughing while you tell it.

You will be stuck paying off your debt with nothing to show for it.

On the upside, many people quit in their first semester because they can get out early with little or no payment. So if you can quit for free, you can always figure out a way to explain away a couple of blank months on your resume. Just remember to delete the phrase *left to attend law school* from the entry on your resume for your last job.

Nonetheless, feeling like a failure might also be a negative ramification.[39]

The alternative is that you stick it out and learn to deal with the stress because it is only a precursor to the stress that you will likely have when you eventually practice law for a living.

When your livelihood depends on your performance or winning a particular case, the stress you have then will be many times greater than just doing well on some exam.

So get out now while you still can retain some dignity.

Besides, most of your fellow students won't remember who you were three years into the future. In their minds, you'll just be known as that nameless person who dropped out first semester.

---

[39] What? You expected some comforting words here?

Or you could learn to deal with the stress by having some fun, watching some movies, or engaging in some activity that is beneficial to your spirit. That would exclude doing drugs, shooting people, and other socially detrimental activities but could include things like going to a party, having consensual sex, playing with Lego, and other socially uplifting activities.

Quiz concerning legal overload

1. Why is burnout bad?
   a. There is nothing good to watch on TV.
   b. A less stupid question might be: Why is the Pope Catholic?
   c. Burnout will prevent you from doing the things you need to do.
   d. Answer C.
   e. Definitely answer C, even though answers A and B are true, but answer D is true, too.

2. What causes burnout?
   a. Law school.
   b. Practicing law.
   c. Anything associated with the law.
   d. Other things.
   e. Definitely answer C, even though answers A and B are true, but answer D is true, too.

3. Match the movie to the stage of depression

Bob Hope's *My Favorite Blonde*	1
The Bourne Identity	2
Airplane	3

4. True or false: Consensual sex is a cure for burnout?
   a. True
   b. False
   c. Neither true nor false.

Quiz Answers

You might have noticed that this chapter had only 3 easy questions. I didn't want you to stress out during this chapter to the point where it would burn you out before you could get to some of the funnier chapters ahead.

1. The correct answer is D.

2. The correct answer is D.

3. I had to make this question a little hard, just to see if you could handle the truth. What do you mean, you can't handle the truth? No, I will not be mentioning any Tom Cruise movies in this book. Just accept the movie cures since they have been scientifically evaluated, and being that science is like a religion, you must believe. The trick I threw in here was in ordering the movies — they don't just line up across. The Bob Hope movie is actually the Stage 3 cure while *Airplane* is a cure at Stage 1. You must have seen *Airplane* already. You could substitute *Office Space* but there is a little too much drama going on in that movie, so stick with *Airplane*.

4. Answer C, neither true nor false. It depends on a lot of factors that you don't want me to bring up now.

Chapter 9 Take-Aways

We can all learn a few things from this chapter even if you aren't overloaded by legal stuff.

1. Burnout is bad.

2. Watching the correct type of movie can cure depression.

3. *Stress* will cause people to drop out of law school, but *Stress* will not give up so easily.

10

Things you don't want to hear the night before the bar exam

The bar exam is unlike any other test you have ever taken. The SAT was important. The LSAT was important. But doing poorly on either of those tests would still leave you with myriad alternatives in your life.

If you did a bad job on the SAT, you probably could take it again or go to a lesser college. If you did poorly on the LSAT, you could take the GRE and pursue a less glamorous field of study but probably one that is more suited to your core spirit.

However, the bar exam is the only test that will make you a real lawyer. Until you pass the bar exam, you really *have* wasted the prior three years. You definitely don't want to stretch it out to wasting four or five years, spending an endless amount of time and money studying for the same test over and over again. Besides wasting time and money, it could also be quite morally draining.

Just to keep the pressure up: don't fail the bar exam!

You could try to pass the bar exam by studying very hard during the bar review class. If you didn't study hard during the bar review class, then you've already failed the bar exam.

But let's say that you did put the work in during the bar review course, there are still things that could derail you.

Failure can come about due to flood, tornado, earthquake, or missing the bus, but it's usually someone you care about that screws it up for you. These failure-inducing events normally come from some close family member or personal friend who brings up the wrong thing at the last minute.

Your soulmate could say, "You don't have a seat number because I forgot to mail those forms for you."

How do you avoid this lovely scenario? First, mail all the forms yourself. Mailing the forms should not be left to husbands who can't remember which day is trash day when it's been the same for the past ten years. It should not be left to girlfriends who borrow your car and never fill up the gas tank. Mailing the forms should never be left to anyone but you.

Of course, in the most technical sense, if someone tells you that they didn't mail in your forms, then you're not taking the bar exam the next day.

What a relief!

However, you will have to take the test someday and better to take it on a day that you prepared for it rather than a half-year later.

If you do want to take the test at the appointed time, you can count on someone giving you disturbing information. Friends and loved ones have all sorts of ways to freak you out.

Here are the top ten things heard by a bar exam test-taker the night before the bar exam:

1. "I've been cheating on you."
2. "I'm pregnant."
3. "I've been cheating on you and I'm pregnant."
4. "We need to talk."
5. "This is more important than some silly test." (Actually that silly test, the bar exam, actually *is* the most important thing happening to you within the next 24 hours.)
6. "You have to study? What about me?!"
7. "I can leave you alone. How about I leave you alone forever."
8. "You've been a failure all your life, why do you think tomorrow will be any different."
9. "You make such a big deal about everything. It's just a test."
10. "I'm okay. I don't want you to worry. But your car

got damaged a little. Yes, a little more than just a little, but you really needed a new car anyway."

Certainly, being told that your spouse has been cheating on you or that your car is now a heap of motionless metal will come as bad news. But you will be taking the most important test of your life tomorrow. What can you do?

You could go back in time and fix things but since the past can only be changed with the use of a time-machine and I doubt that you have a working one available, returning to the past might not be an option.

Maybe you could divide yourself in two or create a duplicate of yourself so that you could take the test while your duplicate will solve all your other problems. Superman tried that but his superpowers were also reduced. Since most wannabe lawyers have limited superpowers to begin with, this solution is probably unavailable to you, too.

You could absorb the bad news by chanting your mantra. However, it may be impossible for you to push disturbing information to the back of your mind.

The best solution to bad news is not to hear it in the first place.

The best solution is to not even hear the bad news in the first place.

A discussion about your rocky relationship or your destroyed car can be enjoyed after the test. And who knows, maybe having such a discussion can save you from having to go on that post-bar exam trip to Europe you had planned.

To avoid delightful phrases, such as "I'm pregnant" or "I'm cheating on you", stay at a hotel and do not tell anyone where you are. It would still behoove you to have the hotel not disturb you or turn off the phone. Thus, you'll avoid the awkward phone call.

Destroy your cell phone, too, because if you just turn it off, you will be tempted to listen to your messages.

If your pregnant girlfriend or your cheating husband are determined to find you, they might. Taking the bar exam in a location near caves in a mountain range is probably the best idea. Hiding in caves has been an effective, time-honored means of avoiding people and, unless your trauma-inducing significant-other  has access to the Marine Corps or to a local sheriff's department, you're probably safe for the evening. Best to choose a cave with electricity, for that one last look at your study sheet.

Hide from friends and loved-ones in a cave.

My own experience was having my girlfriend call to break-up with me the night before I sat for the patent bar. As bar exams go, the patent bar is the most difficult exam I have ever taken. It contains questions such as the following: "If you approach the patent office from the north and desire to enter through the door on the left, which way do you turn the green handle?" Then there are the timing questions such as "If you want to file a patent on a Tuesday, will your have to file it the week following the first of the month."

You probably think that such questions are nonsense. I would agree. However, they *are* that arcane. Studying for a test like that takes some effort. The patent bar also had us write patent claims in a type of obsolete English that lords granting fief to their vassals would think is a bit outdated.

A whole lot of studying goes into one day of your life and having someone interrupt you the night before, especially someone whom you thought was on your side, can be a bit disconcerting.

My miracle was that I was able to put the drama out of my mind and get a good night's sleep because passing the patent bar exam was important for my career. The next morning I got up, went to the testing site, and actually passed the test. The night after the test, she called me back to ask how the test went and to say that she really didn't want to break up with me.

She couldn't have waited a day? One day? Whatever crisis my then-girlfriend was having would still be there the next evening. Why she couldn't see that fact still remains a mystery to me.

I eventually broke up with that girlfriend but not before another two years of my life went by in a continuing psychodrama. That bit of comedy is for another book or TV series.

Perhaps I could recommend that you tell your friends and loved ones not to bother you with any trouble short of imminent death the night before the bar exam.

Instead of psychodrama, have a nice evening.

The night before the New York bar exam, I had dinner with a terrific woman. She offered me uplifting comments, gave me a rose to put on the table when I took the test, and told me to take a chocolate bar to the exam for energy. She was so nice that she didn't want to have dinner with me the night before the exam, not because she knew I was an idiot, but because she thought it might be best for me to make it an early evening.

Knowing I would not get to sleep early the night before the first day of the New York bar exam, I knew that a dinner with her would pave my way to success. Which it did.

However, I was simply lucky beyond belief that evening because uplifting comments the night before the big test don't even make the top 100.

The one thing that most people want to hear before they take a very important test like the bar exam is quite low on the list of things actually heard:

218. "Good luck."

Quiz concerning things you don't want to hear

1. What topic of conversation can wait until after you take the bar exam?
    a. Death.
    b. Pregnancy.
    c. Car accident.
    d. Anything associated with your relationships.
    e. All of the above and everything else you can think of, too.

2. Which of the following would be the best place to stay while you take the bar exam?
    a. Your own home.
    b. The home of a close friend.
    c. A secluded house in the woods.
    d. A cave.
    e. The moon.

3. Why is important not to get bad news the night before you take the bar exam?
    a. You can't handle the truth.
    b. It might distract you from remembering what a tort is when you take the test.
    c. So you don't have anyone but yourself to blame if you do poorly on the test.
    d. You might have enough stress the night before the most important test of your life.
    e. It confirms that you are selfish and uncaring.

Quiz Answers

You can be a good person and still want to avoid getting drawn into discussions about your relationship, your destroyed car, or your shortcomings the night before you take the bar exam. The bar exam is a very stressful test to take and you really don't need more stress. Do you?

1. The correct answer is E because everything will cause you grief the night before the bar exam, even weighing yourself on the scale in your bathroom.

2. This is a bit of a trick question because I said in the chapter that you might want to stay in a cave. However, I said you want to stay in a cave with electricity and most caves are not so equipped. Therefore, the best answer is C, a secluded house in the woods. E is wrong because the moon does not have an atmosphere and is too far away from any of the testing sites.

3. As I mentioned previously, I will not be mentioning any Tom Cruise movies in this book, so answer A is wrong. While you might be selfish and uncaring, you have a good enough excuse the night before the bar exam to want to be alone. Thus, secluding yourself won't prove those shortcomings. Therefore, answer E is wrong. Answers B and C might be true, but answer D is the best answer.

Chapter 10 Take-Aways

Tests are stressful and the bar exam is even more stressful. What you learned from this chapter is that you are entitled to a little "me" time before the test.

1. Your family and friends are just dying to upset you before you take the biggest test of your life because they secretly hate you.

2. Before you take the bar exam, disappear from everyone you know, because they think that whatever is bothering them that evening is more important than you establishing your career.

3. The night before the bar exam it is better to have dinner with someone who says nice things to you than with someone who breaks up with you.

11

The Law Firm Rejection Letter

This chapter will explore a number of creative ways that you can tell a law firm to go to hell when they come knocking at your door.

We have all received rejection letters. The usual scenario consists of an advertised job, an application from a perfectly qualified person, and a rejection letter from the firm to the perfectly qualified person. I suspect that you have been in that position (I'm referring here to you being a perfect match for a job, not being a brutal firm that hands out rejection letters to perfectly qualified candidates).

How about we turn the tables and reject the firms? Why should firms have all the fun sending us letters after they have thought over our qualifications for less than a minute?

That font that you struggled over, that past job that you

spent hours trying to describe, not to mention the experience and education that you actually worked at for years, is all dismissed in seconds as useless, irrelevant, or both.

Law firms produce their own firm resumes, which typically only consist of collections of accolades and honors they bestow upon themselves.

The truth is that the managing partner actually screwed over all those clients he proudly lists. The truth is that the cases won by one great partner really resulted from the effort of 20 associates who got fired after the case ended because the firm could no longer afford them. These truths are not found on the firm resume.

Any elaboration that you made on your resume is of no comparison to the fantasy world of law firm resumes.

When large, supposedly prestigious firms are losing billion dollar cases, you should be asking for writing samples from them. At least ask them why they took the case. If they thought they could win, they were lying. If the knew they would lose, how in good faith could they take their clients' money.

Firms lie. They should be put in their place. Therefore, the renegade attorney should turn the tables on them, pull the chair out from under them, and not give them a key to the bathroom.

How do we turn the tables on these law firms?

We write rejection letters to them.

There are several different types of rejection letters. Although they all basically say that you unfortunately don't want to work for the firm, each has its own way of imparting that message.

We can first start with the simple rejection letter.

The Simple Firm Rejection Letter

In this type of rejection letter, you let the law firm down in one small paragraph.

Dear Firm:

Thank you for your interest in my candidacy for the associate position at your law firm. I have accepted another position but will keep your firm in mind if I should be interested in it in the future.

Sincerely,

The Renegade Lawyer

When you write the letter above, you have taken the simple straightforward approach to the firm. Unfortunately for the firm, you have decided to work elsewhere.

The firm might think that you have accepted a better position, a better firm, or both. Naturally, the firm will be quite disappointed that you rejected it. The firm might go through a real rough patch because it lost such a qualified attorney (you).

Rejection of Firm Because You Receive a Large Number of Inquiries

You might want to placate the firm's anxiety in losing you as a candidate by writing the following letter.

Dear Firm:

Thank you for submitting your firm resume and letter regarding possible employment with your firm.

Unfortunately, my career plans do not make it possible for me to consider your firm at this time. I receive a large number of inquires from highly qualified firms such as yours for a very limited number of persons, namely, one.

I appreciate your interest in me and wish your firm much success in its future endeavors.

Very Truly Yours,

The Renegade Lawyer

Sometimes the firms realize that you have only a limited number of opportunities that you can pursue and actually fill. Usually this limited number is one. More than one job as an attorney, in addition to leading to all sorts of conflicts of interest, will also result in a total lack of sleep and complete mental collapse.

Firms realize that you can only accept one job at a time. Thus, the firm might not feel any better getting a rejection letter that says that you receive a large number of job offers from firms and can only accept one. The firm will know that it does not fare that well in your eyes compared with other firms.

Therefore, it might make sense to be even a bit nicer to the firm you intend to reject because you might want them to approach you again someday for a better or more high-paying job.

Of course, if the firm is so pathetic, you might not want to even write them a letter. But more on total rejection later. For now, let's see how we can let a firm down a bit easier. Easier for them, yet still letting them know that, unfortunately for them, they don't meet your requirements.

Rejection of a Delusional Firm
(Firm thinks it is impressive)

Firms are usually a bit delusional. They think of themselves as impressive entities rather than soldiers for hire (mercenaries). Because they think of themselves in such a grandiose manner, they will accept flattery as truth.

You can use that delusion to your own advantage when you reject a law firm.

You tell them how great they are before you drop the guillotine's blade on their neck (their collective neck).

Dear Firm:

Thank you for your interest in me.

While I find your firm's credentials to be impressive, I am unable to consider working for your firm at this time.

I wish your firm success in finding an applicant who will best appreciate your firm's skills and abilities, and I thank your firm again for its interest in me.

Sincerely,

The Renegade Lawyer

See how in the preceding letter we let the firm down easy. Tell the firm that it is an impressive firm – firms can so easily be depressed. Nothing is worse than a melancholy law firm.

Furthermore, you don't have to come out and say it plainly that while the firm's credentials were impressive, they weren't impressive enough to move you to even consider them. No, all you have to say is that the firm is impressive, and even having said that you still can't work for them.

The firm can go on and think that maybe you have tuberculosis and you don't want to infect such an impressive firm as theirs. On the other hand, when you say the firm is impressive, they might think that you dislike impressiveness and want to work for some poor outfit that has 4 lawyers in a room the size of your bathroom.[40]

It is also polite to wish the firm success in finding someone who might actually want to work for them.

Since very few people might actually like to work for a law firm, saying that you hope they find someone who will appreciate working for their firm means that out of all the people who would hate to work for their firm, you hope that they find someone who hates them less than the rest.

Please also note that the letter thanks the firm twice for their interest in you, once at the beginning and then again at the end. This reiterates the fact that although you find their firm *not impressive enough* and you hope they will find someone who would actually like to work for them, you

---

[40] No matter how large your bathroom is, sticking 4 lawyers in a room that size is dangerous.

deeply appreciate being sought out by them because you value their firm in some *unstated way.*

In most likelihood, that *unstated way* can't be stated because it doesn't exist.

Perhaps you like their décor or the fact that their website is slightly less difficult to peruse through than picking just the right ant to cover in chocolate.

As an aside, some firms are very similar to chocolate covered ants in that they both have disgusting contents covered by something glossy and charging an exorbitant price for the pleasure. Other firms can be compared to rotting bananas but hopefully you get the point.

Returning to the topic of rejecting firms, perhaps you are just not interested in placating or nursemaiding a law firm.

You might have another job or you might be so sick of working as a lawyer that you would rather walk-about in the Australian outback. Whatever the case, politely dismissing a law firm can be the most efficient way of telling them to bugger off.[41]

Rejection Based on Your Anticipated Needs (You Anticipate You Won't Be Needing Them)

When you just want to tell a firm to go away and you don't want to waste ink to puff up their already inflated firm ego, then just tell them that you don't anticipate ever working for them.

---

[41] Britishisms are jolly good.

Dear Firm:

Thank you for sending me your firm resume. I appreciate your interest in me. I have concluded, however, that in light of my anticipated needs, I will not be able to fill your position.

I thank you for your interest in me and wish you the best in the firm's job search.

Very Truly Yours,

The Renegade Lawyer

Quickly and efficiently you have told the firm that you don't need them. Again you have thanked them for sending you their useless firm resume and you thanked them for their interest in you.

You realize of course that their only interest in you was to work you to death to make the most money for the partnership before they can fire you and replace you with a more junior associate.

You also wished them the best in the firm's job search, the best what, though, needn't be spelled out. You might be wishing them the best *nightmare situation* that would make you laugh at them, but they will assume you meant that you wished them the best *success* in their job search.

Not saying something but rather implying the good while secretly meaning the worst is the standard way to write any legal document. Therefore, in these firm rejection letters, you must adopt an attitude of smug superiority while seemingly concerned for their well-being, which of course, you're not.

In most firm rejection letters, therefore, you want to give some indication that you are pleased that the firm was interested in you, but that you have better things to do with your time than to be wrapped up in their petty office politics while being paid less than the market rate from a firm that thinks its name-recognition is so powerful that you would sacrifice all your waking hours making the partners rich.

The "Quick Knife Through the Heart" Rejection Letter

Sometimes, though, a quick knife to the heart, lawyer-style, is the best.

You can dispatch the firm to the oblivion that it deserves with the same amount of compassion that you would squash an insect (not recommended for people concerned about bugs).

Dear Firm:

Thank you for your recent inquiry regarding the opening at your firm. Unfortunately, I am no longer available at this time.

I hope that your firm is able to find a rewarding and successful applicant and I wish it continued success in its legal endeavors.

Very Truly Yours,

The Renegade Lawyer

Short, sweet, and to the point without making a point. You are no longer available. That means that you are not available, at least to them, and how dare they even contemplate that you had even the vaguest interest in being associated with their firm.

The term *unfortunately* means unfortunately for them not for you. This true meaning of *unfortunately* has of late become known to many and so it isn't used as much in rejection letters anymore.

Thus, when you really want to stick it to them, write *unfortunately* and they will know that you have just twisted the knife blade by 90 degrees.

If they don't know it, then all the better for you. The foolish firm will think that you really might have considered working for them. The problem for you will be that sometime in the future, that stupid firm might get it in its collective mind that you would like to consider them again. Hah. The laugh will be on them. Poor stupid firms.

A note on salutations here. *Lawyer-speak* means normally that the more it sounds like you are saying something then the more it is that you are actually saying the opposite.

Thus, it is great to use *Very Truly Yours* for the more flat-out rejections that you must send. *Very Truly Yours* sounds like you are really bound to them and that they can trust you.

Sincerely merely means you are saying what you mean. Thus in a *sincere* letter you have to be quite careful not to convey anything but utter contempt couched in phrases that sound like you are disappointed you can't work for the firm — without actually saying that.

Most times you won't even care if the firm exists past tomorrow let alone whether the firm can find someone to do its dirty work for them.

Nonetheless, since the firm contacted you, you might hope that they find someone who can talk and walk simultaneously while avoiding drooling excessively. Forget about the drooling. Let their new associates drool. It's quite typical for new associates to drool.

The Long Rejection Letter
(Wherein You Appear to Be Explaining
But You Really Aren't)

On occasion, you might want to look like you are explaining (while not really explaining) your reasoning for rejecting the law firm in greater depth.[42]

This way, the law firm will get a longer letter.

A longer letter might imply more actual content and not just a longer brush-off.

A firm receiving a longer letter might be inclined to contact you again in the future after they have gotten their act together and could possibly be worthy enough to contact you.

That's what a longer letters implies.

In reality, you are just writing a longer letter and saying nothing. Lawyers are well trained in writing a lot of words that add up to zero actual content.

Nonetheless, if you want to imply stuff, then go ahead and write that longer letter.

The following letter is an example of the art form of implication without actualization (it implies a lot and says nothing). Don't try to add actual content or real reasoning.

---

[42] Note that I haven't specified what occasion, so it might be Thanksgiving or the birth of a new toad you saw on TV.

That would spoil the whole thing.

Dear Firm:

Thank you for your firm resume and letter expressing interest in me. The information about your firm's qualifications and interests which you have provided me has been carefully reviewed in connection with my present need for a position with a firm like yours. Based upon that review, I have concluded that I will not be accepting an offer of employment from your firm.

In recent years, my popularity has meant that I have received increasingly larger numbers of offers not only from law firms but also from other types of firms that wish to hire me. Practicality requires that I select for further consideration only those firms whose resumes suggest they have the greatest likelihood of meeting my current needs. I must, therefore, decline to accept firms'

> offers despite their distinguished records.
>
> Thank you again for your interest in me. I wish you every success as you seek new associates for your firm.
>
> Sincerely,
>
> *The Renegade Lawyer*

That is an amazing, long, and pompous brush off; just the type of rejection that makes a firm's mouth water (that's the firm's collective mouth).

The letter goes to great lengths to show the firm that you did review their credentials before you rejected them.

Based on that review doesn't offer any reasons for your rejection of the firm. It could be that your review was *hell, no, I'd never work for that firm* or a much more in depth analysis such as *hell, no, I'd never work for that creepy firm.*

Whatever analysis you do, keep it to yourself, because in the end, it's bad news for the poor firm hearing from you. Law firms can be sad and pathetic enough, so there's no need to push them over the edge.

To increase the length of the letter without actually saying anything is not a problem in the legal profession and you should demonstrate it every chance you get — especially in a firm rejection letter.

When you reject a firm, if you want to leave open the option that you might want to work for them in the future, then you have to carefully craft a letter so devoid of substance that they will be dying to have you work for them someday. You can accomplish this desirability with the *pomposity paragraph* (the middle paragraph in the last example letter).

The *pomposity paragraph* inflates your ego, but it also shows the firm that a personage of your caliber gets offers from numerous firms.

Therefore, you are not only choosy by choice but by necessity.

Remember always that a law firm is composed of a lot of people who think they are better than other humans. In ancient times it was the patricians versus the plebeians, but in a law firm it's the partners versus the associates.

When law firm partners read your pompous posturing, they will see it as the same kind of drivel they spew out themselves in their own firm resumes. Thus, they won't hear it as pompous but rather just a straightforward evaluation. The firm will see you as something fantastic and just out of reach: the perfect setting to develop an addictive relationship — where the firm is addicted to you.

If the firm has the gumption to think they are even worthy enough to send you a letter, they are well on their way to begging you to join them in the future.

A firm might like a little rough. But even if you are tempted to spit in their face (the firm's collective face) or on their letter, which probably would be warranted, refrain from the domination game until you have them in leather restraints.

Instead of binding them in leather restraints, send them a rejection letter that says nothing, implies that you would have like to have worked for them but just can't, and is pompous enough so they know it came from a worthy lawyer.

<u>Warning:</u>

Do Not Write Any Law Firm a Rejection Letter

Quiz concerning The Law Firm Rejection Letter

Answer these questions correctly and you could be well on your way to not having a job.

1. What is the major characteristic of a good law firm rejection letter?
    a. Pomposity.
    b. Vacuousness.
    c. The word *unfortunately*.
    d. Rejection.
    e. Silliness.

2. Why use a *pomposity paragraph* to inflate your ego?
    a. So that the firm thinks you are as pompous as it is.
    b. To inflate your ego.
    c. To make you sound grandiose because you are so grand.
    d. Because you can't be considered humble, since *humble* is not a word in the legal lexicon.
    e. So the Prime Directive can be fulfilled.

3. In lawyer-speak, which of the following is the most sincere salutation?
    a. Very Truly Yours
    b. Sincerely
    c. Love always

d. With death wishes

e. SWAK (for "sealed with a kiss")

4. Lawyers have an ingenious way of taking a lot of words and arranging them in order (what we call "sentences"), yet these sentences impart no information. Which of the following is the best example of this lawyerly speech?

a. I need you to know something.

b. When I was three years old, I had a tricycle that was excellent for exploring the world.

c. Global Warming.

d. Read my lips.

e. All the parties agree to the stipulation as entered into before this court.

5. Complete the following analogy: Flattery is to truth as a law firm resume is to _____.

a. your own resume

b. the internet

c. court records

d. flattery

e. truth

6. Why write a rejection letter to a law firm?

a. So that you never get a job with them.

b. Because law firms are insecure and they want to feel like you appreciate them.

     c.   To show them what it feels like to be rejected.

     d.   To prevent them from thinking they are Judge Dredd ("I am the law!").

     e.   To waste time.

7. In rejection letters, what is the hidden message behind the word *unfortunately*?

     a.   It means that something isn't fortunate.

     b.   It's like sticking the knife blade in deep and then twisting it.

     c.   There is no hidden message.

     d.   The hidden message is a secret, so it cannot be divulged.

     e.   Energy equals the product of mass and the square of the speed of light.

Quiz Answers

This chapter was written for your enjoyment, not for you to be writing rejection letters to law firms. Please keep that concept in your mind as you review your answers.

1. Although it is good to be pompous in a rejection letter, answer A is not the correct answer because you don't have to be pompous. Answer B is incorrect because you don't want your letter to be empty; you want it to be full of rejection. Thus, answer D, rejection, is the correct response. Answer C is wrong since we know from being crafty lawyers that the word *unfortunately* does not need to appear in the letter. And, always remember, it is unfortunate for them. Answer E is wrong because silliness refers to the chapter, not to the content of the letter.

2. Answer E can be eliminated immediately because the Prime Directive refers to the rule that the Federation cannot interfere in the internal affairs of member planets. This is a directive that is constantly violated by the Federation and its representatives aboard the starship Enterprise. The directive does not apply to law firms or letters directed to them. Answer D is wrong because humbleness is relative in the legal profession, though it is correct that humble is not in the legal lexicon. Answer C is wrong because although you are grand, you are not

being pompous to show your grandness. Your grandness is evident no matter what you do.[43] Answer B is wrong because you are humble and grand, and your ego is just fine. In fact you don't even need to look at the diet chapter because you don't need to lose weight. You look marvelous. Since you now know all the wrong responses, the correct response is obvious to you (it's answer A). You want the firm to think you are as pompous as the firm is because then the firm will feel a sense of communion or oneness with you. Then you can create a sick, codependent relationship with the firm.

3. The answer is E, sealed with a kiss, because that kiss could be the kiss of death or the impassionate kiss that you have wanted to give all you life. Thus, whether you meant it in the worst or the best sense, it was sincere. Answer D is wrong because death wishes would mean collecting less money because you always want to get emotional damages and you can't get emotional damages from a corpse. Answer C is wrong because it might not be true love, but just a ploy to get you to stipulate to something. Answers A and B are wrong because answer E is more righter.[44]

---

[43] This is an example of flattery, which will be important in another question.

[44] This isn't proper English; I'm having fun making up words.

4. While all the answers to this question truly say nothing, only answer A is correctest.[45]

5. In this question, a law firm resume is equated to flattery and you must pick which of the answers could stand in for the truth. Since your resume is packed with lies, too, answer A is incorrect. Answer B — don't make me laugh out loud (LOL). Answer E might make the sentence true but it's not elegant enough for a test like this. Answer D has possibilities because it would mean that a law firm resume is as far away from flattery as flattery is from the truth, but then you get into relativistic physics and Einstein wouldn't approve. Answer C is correct because there is always a court reporter there. You can hire a court reporter yourself if you are ever having an argument with your significant other and you need to have the truth recorded.

6. E, to waste time. Don't send rejection letters to law firms; they won't appreciate them.

7. Reading comprehension folks; see pages 175 - 176. Answer B.

---

[45] *Ibid.*

Chapter 11 Take-Aways

Rejection letters suck, especially when you get them. Maybe law firms should feel that same sort of rejection.

1. *Unfortunately* is fortunate for you if you're the one who gets to write *unfortunately*.

2. Words written by lawyers can have more than one meaning.

3. In a rejection letter, kind words are just a distraction from the impending knife to the jugular.

4. Law firms have been having all the fun writing you rejection letters. Now it's time for you to have the fun.

5. Law firm rejection letters, written by you and sent to law firms, will make you laugh until you find out that you can't get a job anywhere because the law firms have blacklisted you.

Special Exercise & Special Warning

If you have ever applied for a job, chances are that you have received a rejection letter. For this special exercise, pick a firm that rejected you and write your own rejection letter to them.

Let this be a cathartic experience. It would most likely be unwise for you to actually send a rejection letter to a firm.

Firms like to be in control. If you have the chutzpah to send a firm a rejection letter, the firm would probably not take too kindly to receiving such a letter. In fact, the firm might go out of its way to destroy you. Destruction could come in the form of being blacklisted by the legal profession forever or Bruce Willis might stand behind you yelling Yippee Kai Aye....

Therefore, while law firm rejection letters might seem like a good idea, in reality they're not.

I just wanted to clear that up for you in case you had any questions, doubts, or really stupid plans to send rejection letters to law firms and destroy your career.

12

Law Firm Culture

ard work — that's what America and the Dark Ages were built on. There is a reason why those serfs of the 1200s never lived past 40 and it's the same reason why so many attorneys have heart attacks around the same time: owing fief to the nobles.

That might take some explaining.[46]

Most lawyers are part of a pyramid scheme we call a *law firm*. In this *law firm* there are the nobles, referred to as *the partners*, lesser nobles referred affectionately to as *the junior partners* and a whole array of serfs, affectionately called *associates*.[47]

---

[46] It does take explaining, but please don't expect much from the explanation.

[47] You might argue that the secretaries and the staff are the serfs, but we're talking about the legal hierarchy here. As we will see, these poor folks are even further down the totem pole. Most likely the part of the pole buried deep in the ground.

As an associate, your life becomes dependent on fulfilling the partners' wishes. The laws of time and motion are irrelevant. If a partner wants a brief drafted by Tuesday, then by golly, you better have that draft by Tuesday even if it is impossible.

Case in point, as an intellectual property attorney I had to do review some technology that our law firm's client wanted to buy. Friday at 3 p.m., 25 books on java (the computer language not the island nor the coffee beans) were dumped on my office floor. I had to do this review over the weekend because the partner wanted it done by Monday. It would take weeks to just compare the pictures in the books to targeted technology.

Most law firm partners are unaware of the limitations imposed by the laws of physics.

No time machine was available. No wizardlike ability to bend space. The partner wanted it on Monday and that was that.

Therefore, one of the most interesting things that attorneys and especially partners in law firms think is that it is possible to defy the laws of physics. The classic is the attorney who wants something done in an impossible time span.

When I was a young associate, a partner wanted help on a document project. In the old days, this involved checking things off on forms showing who sent what to whom, whether the document was relevant, and, if so, why. A number of other things to look for, too, but you get the idea. Being in a position to turn it down if I didn't think I had the time (which is a good position to be in — the ability to refuse work; and by the way, only accept duty on a document review project if your brain has stopped working).

I did a quick time and motion check because the partner in charge said she wanted a box of documents done a day. I calculated that it would take at least 30 seconds to complete a form for the most irrelevant of documents. Longer still if the document reviewed was relevant.

One of those legal sized boxes can contain 3000 pages. That can be 10 copies of a 300-page contract, or 3000 one-page letters. 3000 times a half-minute is 1500 minutes or 25 hours, which is 4 workdays. So one box could take anywhere from a few minutes (for those photocopies of the 300-page contract) to 4 days (for all those letters).

I went to the partner with my calculations to make sure that she meant on average that she wanted a box of documents done a day. No, she wanted a box a day. Then she showed me a chart she kept of everyone's progress. Some people were way out ahead and some had fallen behind dramatically. I suggested the disparity might be because the boxes were so dissimilar. She did not want to hear what I had to say on the subject. Needless to say, I declined the invitation to work for her.

**Partners have no magical powers,
but they think they do.**

She had demonstrated no magical powers to bend time and space. She did not look like Scotty from Star Trek and she obviously didn't have the mind of Mr. Spock. She didn't have a wormhole or even the knowledge of the Ancients. In short, she had no control of time or space to be able to will someone to get a box a day done. As a renegade, I have special powers, but only on computer driven document reviews, not when checking off paper. Besides, I hate papercuts.

And I did have other work to do. I had to help my brother paint his apartment.

Most of the time you won't be able to refuse to do the work and you definitely won't be able to avoid the unrealistic deadlines.

Law School might be relevant after all.

In law school, the arbitrary deadlines seem, well, arbitrary. That's because they are. In law school you'll think that it is ridiculous that they assign such arbitrary deadlines.

Now you learn the truth. Working in a law firm is actually worse than law school.

In law school, there is some semblance of camaraderie because everyone seems to complain that the work is just stressful nonsense and the deadlines are just there to make your life miserable. In a law firm, only the lucky few will be able to commiserate with their fellow associates. And please, don't ever even think about commiserating with any of the partners.

Those who are about to die
salute you.

Partners can have as much compassion or consideration as the owner of a gladiator school in ancient Rome.

Let's imagine that I worked for one of those monster law firms in Manhattan where I luckily served a very nice partner as my lord and master. Because I was interested in the business side of intellectual property, I was willingly loaned to another mighty lord. However, unknown to both me and my noble, this business partner was one of those screaming nuts, who was so self-important that he thought he should be king, if not something much more elevated.[48]

Nevertheless, I attempted to fulfill his needs.[49]

Once, I had to sit through an 8-minute tirade of his on the intra-office phone, yelling at me that he wanted a particular piece of information in a memo that I wrote for him. Unfortunately for me, it took me 8 minutes to get through his screaming to tell him it was in the memo, the middle of the second page to be exact.[50]

I could hear him on the phone ask another associate (a backstabbing wench) in his office if my assertion was true. When she meekly answered yes, the partner told me okay and hung up.

---

[48] Naturally, I'm referring to a totally fictitious screaming nut.

[49] Legal needs, as in legal work, nothing else.

[50] The memo was 5 pages total. I should have realized that many partners can't read more than a paragraph or two.

Return to the Dark Ages.

Ahhhh, the joys of the 13th Century. Sure it wasn't like being flogged for no reason. There was no blood of mine spilled on the floor. But, if you weren't a renegade and were the type of person who would take such a partner seriously, then ulcers and high blood pressure would be your reward. Nevertheless, it is hard not to take the situation seriously. It seems that the daily life in a law firm is still reminiscent of the 1200s.

However, you might want to characterize the law firm environment as ancient Rome, but that would be too glamorous. The togas, the orgies, and the *pax romana* were far more fantastic than anything the modern law firm can deliver.

There is a cultural divide.

Certain partners might seem friendly but there is still that cultural divide — something unlike anything we've ever experienced in our American life. The caste system of the law firm is ever present. Nothing will break through it. Again, I have been quite lucky in my career in working for a number of partners who were actually nice human beings. Have I lived the exception?

Why should this caste system continue? That question is almost like asking why does the bar exam still exist.

The bar exam only makes it harder for anyone to practice law. During any particular exam sitting in

California, usually more than half the test takers fail the exam. The answer is simply, "if I had to go through that then so should you." What a lovely attitude.

That same attitude permeates the law firm environment. Young attorneys must be broken in. In some way, it is good training for the inevitable cycle of winning and losing that an attorney will be going through. However, if the whole system were a bit nicer, then that kind of torture would not be needed at all.

In a recent phone conversation with the hiring attorney at one of the largest and most prestigious Australian law firms, I was told that their firm hesitates to hire American attorneys because they are so combative. Imagine a legal system that doesn't treat people like jerks so as to produce jerks. Impossible? Perhaps. But it looks like they are going for a bit friendly route down under.

But we're not down under. We are he in the good ol' US of A, remembering not to smile in the hallways, not enjoying our lives, and definitely not rocking the legal boat. Unless you're a renegade.

The power lies below.

If you can tie into the staff's newswire, you will learn an awful lot more than what you get from the other attorneys and especially the partners. On the other hand, that obligates you to inform the staff and especially the secretaries with juicy gossip that you come across regarding the other attorneys.

The secretary that is always extremely powerful is the head partner's secretary (you can also substitute the secretary for the partner whom you work for, as they will certainly be higher up on the ladder than you). The reason why this lead secretary is so powerful is because they are the gatekeeper to your boss. This a concept lost on many attorneys.

Upstairs, downstairs

or

Talking in front of the hired help.

Secretaries see everything. They are treated like second or third class citizens in most law firms because they will never be at the level of human development that the lawyers will be at, or at least that is what a lot of lawyers think.

When they have one of those movies about ancient Rome and the patricians are going on about their troubles and intrigues and discussing these things right in front of the servants — that's the feeling I get with attorneys and their secretaries.

After talking to many secretaries on this subject of second-class citizenship status, they all tell me that the young attorneys are the worst. Worse still are those attorneys who went directly from college to law school and then to their first attorney job because they most likely never had to work in a real world environment and so haven't learned the rudiments of interpersonal conduct. The lawyer thinks that they are great and that the rest of the world must know of that greatness.

I was at a firm Christmas party when one of the older secretaries told me to stop talking to her and go talk to the partners to make some points. The renegade might not think politically, but never forget that a law firm is like a mini Roman Empire. The lawyers are the patricians, the paralegals are the plebeians, and the staff are the servants.

Give unto Caesar
that which is Caesar's.

The infallibility syndrome goes further. Never forget who is a partner in a law firm and who is merely an associate.

Certainly nowadays in the cutthroat world of the law, partners are fired as easily as associates. Also, there are different grades of partner, equity and nonequity. Equity partners are the real partners. They have paid into the firm and thus own a piece of the action.

Nonequity partners are people who are too senior to be associates but the partnership doesn't really want them as full partners. So the nonequity partner doesn't have to pay anything in, but still has all the liability attached to the partnership (should the lofty firm be sued for malpractice or something else nefarious). While nonequity partners might eventually become full partners, you can still regard them as pathetic and laugh at them behind their backs. Full partners can be regarded as more evil.

So while every Senator in ancient Rome thought that he should be Emperor, only people of the ilk of Caesar or

Pompeii were at the top of the ladder (yes, I know they are from the days of the Republic but it's still a good analogy to make such an important point).

My advice to the renegades out there is to treat the staff nicely and regard the partners with suspicion. You might also want to be nice to the partners and regard the staff with suspicion.

Quiz concerning Law Firm Culture

Law firms have their own culture. See if you can survive in it by answering the questions below correctly.

1. Based on the information in this chapter, what is the best analogy to the modern American law firm?
    a. The 13th Century Dark Ages.
    b. Ancient Rome (Republic or Empire).
    c. Virgin Megastores
    d. Wal-Mart
    e. Answers A and B.

2. Of the following, who has the most power in a law firm?
    a. Whoever knows Harry Potter or can perform feats of magic.
    b. The partners.
    c. The Nonequity partners.
    d. Scotty or Spock, depending on the episode.
    e. The secretaries.

3. Whom should you regard with suspicion in a law firm?
    a. Partners.
    b. Secretaries.
    c. Nonequity partners.
    d. Paralegals.
    e. Everyone.

4. Whom should you be nice to in a law firm?

    a. Partners.

    b. Secretaries.

    c. Nonequity partners.

    d. Paralegals.

    e. Everyone.

Quiz Answers

Hopefully this chapter and the little quiz will help you fit into law firm culture a bit easier.

1. Of course the answer is A, because the Romans were more scientifically advanced than the people of the Dark Ages, so that *defying the laws of physics* stuff has more in common with the alchemy of the Middle Ages. On the other hand, that Roman stuff did sound good, so maybe B is the correct answer. But they both sound so good; maybe E is the best answer. Whatever. I have no idea what happens in Wal-Mart or those Virgin Megastores. They weren't in the reading anyway. Don't sweat this question because no one in the law firm will care. And now I'm leaning to the Roman Empire analogy.

2. The partners (the real partners, not the non-equity partners), so answer B is the correct answer.

3. Answer E.

4. Answer E.

Chapter 12 Take-Aways

Before you join a law firm, it would be wise to reread this chapter and understand law firm culture so you won't be afraid.

1. Working as a new associate at a law firm is like being kicked really hard in the spleen. Unfortunately, if your spleen ruptures, you could die very quickly. Therefore, you have to protect your spleen with iron and steel.

2. The culture of a law firm is either like Ancient Rome or like the Dark Ages in Europe in the 13th century. It could also be like the Klingon Empire (without the bumpy foreheads).

3. Secretaries possess valuable information.

4. Partners think they can defy the laws of physics and conquer time and space.

13

The Evil of Overbilling

Picture a law firm with two men in neighboring offices. One is fat and one is skinny. We will call the fat one *Hamburger* and the thin one *Hotdog*.

Hamburger comes in an hour later and leaves an hour earlier than Hotdog every single day. Hotdog runs around the office and not only appears very busy but actually *is* very busy. Hotdog is stressed but usually in an upbeat mood.

Hamburger sits in his office most of the day and when he comes out he always has a worried look on his face, which, as we know from an old Seinfeld episode, gives everyone in the office the impression that he is working on something important.[51]

I went into Hamburger's office one day to ask him a

---

[51] George worked for the Yankees and looked upset all the time.
As we all know, George wasn't working very hard at the Yankees
– and neither was Hamburger at this old law firm.

question. Please note that I didn't go to see Hamburger because I thought he had any knowledge that I or anyone else could actually use. I was told to ask him.

There was that lazy, fat, good-for-nothing, oh, yes, I should refer to him as Hamburger, sitting there with his feet up on the desk reading the newspaper. Reading his newspaper!

I interrupted him.

The reason I didn't like this idiot (as if I needed more of a reason) was because while he was in the office two hours less each day than Hotdog, he billed two hours more a day than Hotdog did!

I know this because all the secretaries hated him and loved me and when they had to type in the two different time sheets from the two attorneys, one of the secretaries asked me how this could possibly be correct that Hamburger could bill two hours a day more than Hotdog yet work two hours less a day.

Have you guessed it yet?

No, it's not because he did work on the train, or on a bus, or at home.

It was because we were all working on one case and Hotdog wrote *The case 8.5 hours*. Whereas Hamburger, also working on only the one case, broke everything he did (or rather didn't do) into many parts. So he had *Phone conference 0.2* and *Reviewed memo 1.9* and so on, adding up to over 10 hours on the same day that he worked two hours less than Hotdog did!

An exact reproduction of their timesheets follows:[52]

Billable Hours Time Sheet Comparison

Hotdog		Hamburger	
Research of case law, analysis of pleadings, review of deposition transcript, review of memo, phone conferences.	8.5	Research	2.3
		Reviewed memo	1.9
		Analysis of pleading	2.1
		Review of deposition transcript	2.6
		Phone conference	0.2
		Attorney conference	0.3
Total	8.5	Total	10.5

---

[52] Exact in the sense that it helps make my point (so it's not really exact).

He even billed the *Conference* that he had with me. *Conference*! We talked for no more than a minute and he billed it as a *Conference* at 0.3 hours. That's 18 minutes in human time.

Please, attorneys reading this book; be honest with your timesheets.

Of course Hamburger was able to meet his billable hours requirement; but one day he will be found out and exposed for the bill-padding fraud that he is.[53]

Lying about your billable hours is not a good thing.

I particularly didn't like Hamburger, not only because he was a liar and a cheat, but because he had written a memo, all of 3 pages long, that summarized one aspect of the law in a way that would lose the case for us (a very big case).

When I brought it to the attention of the partner in charge, he was as horrified as I was. Thankfully I was lucky enough to work for some really good people. I suggested that I look for any alternate theories that would support our side of the case and the partner agreed. I later produced a 50-page memorandum that had all the alternatives we needed.

What I could never understand, and what the secretaries remarked at, was why Hamburger was still employed and why did the partners even ask him questions.

There are so many aberrant personalities in the law, that

---

[53] For liability reasons, Hamburger is totally fictitious.

I really cannot understand how they all remain employed unless those they work for have even more aberrant personalities. Thus, Hamburger must be just one of the crowd.

Perhaps he stayed around because he dressed well. Hotdog wasn't married and you could tell that when he came into the office there was no one at home giving him the *once-over* before he left for work to make sure that his tie didn't clash with his suit or that his collar was sitting down properly around his tie.

Hamburger was married to another hamburger. Another lawyer in the office caused a minor embarrassment when she met Mrs. Hamburger and asked her if she was pregnant. She wasn't. Anyway, Mrs. Hamburger had good taste in clothes and was able to make Hamburger look presentable.

Poor Hotdog, no clothes consultant for him.

So what happened? Was Hamburger exposed for timesheet fraud? Would anyone ever realize that Hotdog, although not as snappy a dresser, actually had the substance and integrity to be a really good lawyer?

Two points to address when answering those questions. First, you always have to wonder whether law firms appreciate timesheet fraud because it makes them more money.[54]

Overbilling was how they busted that crooked law firm in one of those Tom Cruise movies that I won't be discussing. Of course in the real world things like that never

---

[54] I'm not accusing anyone. Just wondering out loud.

happen.

Second, the idea that substance and integrity are pluses in the legal profession, well, I think I'll leave that topic alone because we're looking for funny stuff here, not serious soul-searching questions.

Besides, that whole huge firm disintegrated, so we'll never know what happened.[55]

Beware of lawyers who appear to worry too much.

The lawyer who looks like he is always worrying is actually not worrying; he only looks like it. He is hoping that everyone else will worry. That way, no one will ever suspect that he has no idea what he is doing.

At one fictitious firm where I worked, we had a fictitious guy like this who was such a classic tool that you could start conversations with strangers by simply mentioning this guy. Anyone who had ever encountered him realized almost instantly how annoying he is. I have never met anyone who liked him.

How did he stay employed if everyone disliked him?

There were many times when the partners would berate him for being a dumb oaf, annoying jerk, wrong loser, or just stupid idiot. I think the reason is because when *Stress* is your constant companion, sometimes it is just convenient to have

---

[55] And the author has no intention of finding out. Besides, these are all fictitious people — definitely fictitious — at a fictitious firm.

someone to yell at.[56]

It made my life easier because he was around. Since no one liked him, I would get my mail from the mailroom faster and my documents typed by the wordprocessing staff sooner.

The worrier creates a lot of busy work and while that might work with some clients, someday some wise client will object.

The double-biller is a variant on the worrier. Lawyers bill their time, some lucky ones by the quarter hour, but most by the tenth of an hour. Every six-minute interval should be charged to some client or someone won't be getting a bonus at the end of the year.

Classic double-billing, which is not a problem, is sitting on a plane for one client and doing work for another — a great way to bill twice for the time on the same trip. This type of situation has become the basis for jokes about lawyers not getting into heaven because they have billed more hours per day than exist in a day. In reality, though, the attorney is doing work for two clients at the same time. Thus, the joke, while possibly funny, is not a flaw.

Bad double-billers bill two clients while doing work for neither.

The real pain in the rumpus double-biller is the attorney who constantly second-guesses previous decisions and

---

[56] See the concluding chapter, wherein I discuss *Stress* as your constant companion.

forces everyone else to go back do some work again. This means, he reads your memo and thinks you missed something but doesn't know what, so you have to do it again. Or you just finished a review of documents (and what fun that is) and the double-biller comes along and says that he thinks something else should be looked for in the same documents.

Yes, you will make your billable hour requirement for the year with this guy around and the partnership probably loves him for sucking all that money out of the client and into the law firm. However, you will not get any valuable experience out of it, the extra work will be pointless, and it always looks like you didn't do a good job in the first place when it really is the double-biller just screwing around. It is a form of covert-aggression.

Covert-aggressors have the knack to make you look like you are the guilty party while they are the innocent rose. The worrier does this by being all worried. You're not worried? The worrier is worried and will go tsk-tsk at anyone who doesn't show the kind of concern he shows.[57]

That one pest I referred to earlier was so busy pretending to worry that he never had time to clean up his office. When a date would meet me at the law firm, his office was always on the tour because it was a nightmare and smelled bad, too.

Just remember that all these characters are a lot more than nuisances. They are a way to break the ice with people and to have someone to make fun of.

---

[57] Don't forget, he's just showing worry he doesn't really care.

Quiz concerning the evil of overbilling

Be a good lawyer and turn away from the dark side of overbilling evil.

1. What would you do if you had a project to review documents for topic A and topic B?
    a. Worry about it on the outside, and not care about it on the inside.
    b. Go through the documents to spot topic A, and then go through them all again for topic B, and then go through them again for topic A, and then go through them again for a new topic C.
    c. Bill the client for going through the documents before you look at the documents and then go through them separately for each topic A and B, and then again for fictitious topic C.
    d. Go through the documents for topics A and B.
    e. Sit in your office and read the newspaper.

2. If you have a telephone conference with someone concerning your case, how much do you bill the client for if you were on the phone for 5 minutes?
    a. 0.2 hours
    b. 0.1 hours
    c. 0.3 hours

d.   1.2 hours if the phone call was an incoming
     call from someone other than the client
e.   0.4 hours

Quiz Answers

Hopefully you got this chapter's extremely complex ethics questions correct.

1. The correct answer is D. The other answers are wrong. Hopefully you didn't pick any wrong answer.

2. The answer is B because 0.1 hours is 6 minutes. You bill the amount you work to the next nearest tenth of an hour. Since 0.1 hours is 6 minutes and you worked 5, then 0.1 would be the proper amount. Answer A, 0.2 hours, is too much, as is answer C, 0.3 hours. Answer E is way too much and answer D is ridiculous.

Chapter 13 Take-Aways

Overbilling your client is not a nice thing. Here are some pointers you can hold dear, so that you remain an ethical lawyer.

1. Bill you client for the amount of time you worked for him not the amount that your Ojai board suggests.

2. If you must worry about a case, worry on the inside and not on the outside. Definitely don't be the type of person who worries on the outside and not on the inside just to make it seem like you are more concerned with winning the case than everyone else because soon everyone will realize that you are a real tool if you do that, so don't do it.

3. Be efficient.

4. Don't be a dork.

14

Lawyer Style

If your firm has a formal dress-code then it will be much easier to buy clothes. The suit, uniform for both men and women, is so standard that when I went to a movie audition years ago where I had to bring some of my own clothes, the head of the wardrobe department said to me, "these look like lawyers clothes."

The head of the wardrobe department was correct. I was a lawyer and those were my clothes. What distinguished them from MBA suits or a manager of geologists? I haven't quite figured it out. Perhaps it was because I had such high quality fabrics. I'm just joking there, but who knows. The wardrobe head couldn't really place a finger on what made them lawyer's suits either, but lawyer's suits they certainly were.

If the dress-code at your law firm calls for suits, you can just go to wardrobe and ask them to pull the appropriate clothes.[58]

If, however, you have to develop a style and panache all your own that says casual with style, most lawyers will be in trouble.[59]

What Not To Wear

The *bowtie and suspenders* guy is a classic geek.

With only a bowtie, a guy is just a nerd. He probably knows a lot about a very obscure subject area and doesn't know how to talk to girls.

With just suspenders (and a regular tie), a guy is usually just a fat guy who needs to hold up his pants.

But the *bowtie and suspenders* guy is the one who really thinks he knows a lot about the most important issues of the day and he wants everyone to believe that premise. Unfortunately, he know far less than the nerd and even far less than the fat guy.[60]

The BS (*bowtie and suspenders*) guy tries to make up for his lack of knowledge and finesse with arrogance and a loud voice.

Contrary to what you have seen of many lawyers,

---

[58] Of course you will have to wear suits all the time, so you might want to pray that your law firm has a *casual* dress code.

[59] Mastering casual style correctly is definitely painful, so you might want to pray that your law firm has a *formal* dress code.

[60] The fat guy is probably very educated and has just been sitting and reading too much.

arrogance and a loud voice are actually not substitutes for knowledge. I know — it's a shock.

The woman who wears sweat-clothes – if she's an attorney, she won't be working for the firm for too long, so no need to make her acquaintance.

If she's a paralegal, she won't be working for the firm for much longer, so no need to make her acquaintance. If she's a secretary, she probably doesn't do a whole lot of work, so bring your work to the person who is dressed more businesslike. That person might do just a little work and not well, but everyone will have a bit more respect for them and so their work will seem better even with 20 extra typos.[61]

If you are confronted with a male attorney wearing sweatpants or a female attorney wearing a bowtie and suspenders, then pray that they are opposing counsel and not partners from your main office.

Imitation is the sincerest form of flattery

Lawyers at entertainment law firms love to develop their own style which looks very similar to the style of their clients. Collarless shirts, Nehru jackets, vests with asymmetric buttoning will immediately tell the crowd that you are part of the _business_ as it is referred to in Los Angeles.[62]

As an aside, I have to comment on the number of

---

[61] At 21 typos, though, even that secretary will need a new job, too.

[62] There's no business like show business.

lawyers in Los Angeles who have nothing to do with the entertainment industry but refer to entertainment people by their first names as if they just bonded with them after a tough deposition or extravagant lunch (the *have your people call my people* type of lunch).

Usually, their only contact with the entertainment industry is attending a premier at a movie studio because one of their friends who works there got them tickets. The event they were attending was likely canceled.

New York is a bit more conservative, so nix the asymmetric vests. In New York, it's not the *movie types* that dominate the legal business but rather the *money people*. That is why in Los Angeles, you will see lawyers dressed for an episode of the Jetsons while in New York City, most of the lawyers are dressed to imitate bankers and money managers. Typically, bankers and money managers do not dress flashy.

In the rest of the country, you will be known as a freak. If you have to explain that you are an entertainment lawyer in Biloxi, Mississippi, and that is the reason you are wearing an asymmetric vest, then it's time to move or just admit you are a medical malpractice attorney with flair.

Dressing Down

Speaking of flashy, if you like trendy clothes, or even clothes that look good, avoid insurance companies.

I was waiting for an interview once at an insurance company and as I sat and watched the lawyers passing by, I knew I wouldn't get the job. Every single one of the attorneys, man or woman, had on a blue suit. I didn't, and still don't, own a blue suit.

At another insurance company I had to take a personality test. Dumb questions like if you are sitting on a bus, whom would you sit next to: the construction worker, the clown, or the veterinarian? Deep psychological insights can be gleaned from your answer to that question. Yeah, sure.

Although I answered all the dumb questions as honestly as possible. When they came back with the results they wondered aloud if I had answered the questions honestly since my results fell outside their range. If you fall outside the insurance company's parameters then you have to be lying. I wonder if that maxim holds true for those height/weight charts.

I need to face it; I'm not meant to work in an insurance company. That shouldn't stop you if you have a plain blue suit and you need a job. Just watch out. If you're a renegade, your personality won't fall into their range. If you want to be a renegade, then burn that blue suit, unless it has a Nehru jacket.

Dressing for crime

Criminal defense attorneys also seem to want to dress like their clients: a little too formal. All very nice, but looking a little like the wardrobe manager was dressing them for something other than the law. Men with cufflinks and very expensive suits, pinstripes with too much space between each stripe. Women with small black dresses, reminiscent of the mob-boss girlfriend type.

Criminal prosecutors aren't making enough money to worry about their wardrobe. The ones who are worrying about their wardrobes are the sons and daughters of the super-wealthy who are doing the public a service by contributing to the public good. These lawyers are just working on a lark, so they have plenty of time to worry about their wardrobe — and do.

Please note that someone working as a lawyer just for the fun of it might not suffer the same degree of stress as the rest of us because the fallback position for them — running their family business or just cruising around on the family yacht — is always in the back of their minds.

Out of Uniform

As a renegade you might think that you will have to wear outrageous clothes or do something extreme.

The extreme I went to as a first year attorney was to toss my tie over my shoulder as I read cases in books in the firm's library.

Perhaps you won't work with a firm with a library. Perhaps you'll do all your research online.[63]

Perhaps you won't have to wear a tie at work. In each of those situations, there might be something analogous.

Nevertheless, renegade status comes easily by just doing

---

[63] That's a mistake. Read a book!

something that makes your life merely incrementally easier.

When reading a book while wearing a tie, the tie has the audacity to get in between the pages. You could tuck the tie down under the book, but I was wearing some nice expensive ties and I didn't want to ruin them.[64]

Thus, I took the outrageous action of flipping my tie up over my shoulder.

That's nothing, you say.

Wrong!

From the reactions I got, you would think that I had been walking around the law firm in my pajamas.

A tie over the shoulder equals out of uniform. Only try that if you are a certified renegade.

I was questioned as to whether or not the library was windy.

Where were the gusts coming from?

Do I really think I should do that with my tie?

Why was I doing that?

That last question seemed like an invitation to explain my outrageous behavior. It seemed like that to me, but it was really just a way for that partner to have confirmation that I just wasn't fitting into the legal square hole. I was illustrating for everyone that I was a round peg.

In the end, there was no way to avoid the tie incidents because I wasn't going to sacrifice my ties for the sake of the firm's library. Besides, I was only doing this while reading

---

[64] You never know what's on or in one of those casebooks. Forget it; do your research online.

casebooks. I wasn't doing it while clients or the general public were about the place.

That is how a renegade thinks: if it really does not matter, then it should not matter.

However, you will find some legal professionals are so hung up on nonsense that they will take things that don't matter and make an issue out of it.

Nitpicking is the technical term.

Nitpicking seems to grow exponentially in the law firm setting. The reason being that with the critical mass of all those attorneys in one place, nitpicking takes on new dimensions, namely, nitpicking on things that don't even matter.

I should admit that I like to kick it up a notch. At a large Los Angeles firm I worked for, we could be sure that the clients and the almost all the staff would clear out by 5 p.m. That being the case, I would shed my shoes for comfortable slippers.[65]

Wearing slippers might be pushing the envelope a bit too far.

You might think that wearing slippers is pushing this *renegade thing* a bit, but the best is yet to come.

Naturally, even late into the evening, I am not the only

---

[65] Damn it. If I'm staying late every evening of every working day and coming in on the weekends every weekend, I'm going to be a little comfortable when I have the opportunity.

attorney in the office. The partner I was working for called me down to his office to discuss a case I had to go to court on the next day. After we finished our discussion and another attorney popped in while we were standing up, my partner noticed I was wearing nonstandard footgear.

"Are those slippers?" he asked in a kind of puzzlement.

I explained my reasoning as I did above to you.

At that explanation, he shook his head and was about to say something that I knew would involve some phrase stating that slippers might not be appropriate for the legal community even in an office with nobody in it.

So I preempted him and agreed not to leave my office without proper shoes on.

Sometimes a renegade has to retreat lest he loses his job

over such minor issues.

Luckily for me I worked for a nice partner who could live with a little quirkiness. Although I still stand by my slippers, the slipper incident became a nice issue for my contemporaries to tease me about for years to come.[66]

---

[66] And now you can, too.

Quiz concerning lawyer style

Without an assigned uniform, sometimes it is difficult to decide what to wear to work. If you are a lawyer, then that decision-making process can be even more difficult because the practice of law can dwell on appearances. Answer the questions below to see if you have the right fashion sense for a law firm.

1. What should you not wear to a law firm?
   a. Sweats.
   b. Bowties.
   c. Slippers.
   d. Orange prison uniforms.
   e. All of the above.

2. If you wanted to work for an insurance company, what should you wear to your interview?
   a. A flashy red suit.
   b. Slippers.
   c. Bowties and suspenders.
   d. A cheap blue suit.
   e. An asymmetrical shirt from the trendiest fashion house in your city.

3. Which of the suits depicted on the next page would be the best option for a man to wear to an interview at a law firm?

a.

b.

c.

d.

e.

4. What is the major difference between the clothes that a lawyer wears as opposed to clothes worn by people in other professions?

    a. A lawyer's clothes can be determined to be such by experienced movie studio wardrobe heads.

    b. A lawyer's clothes are more impressive.

    c. Lawyers dress like their clients.

    d. Lawyers own a lot more blue suits.

    e. Everything lawyers wear is asymmetrical.

Quiz Answers

They (whoever they are) say that you can't judge a book by its cover. That is totally irrelevant for this quiz, but can you judge lawyers by their clothes? Check below to see if you can.

1.   This question had a lot to do with whether you read the chapter and not so much with reality. Nonetheless, you really shouldn't wear any of the items mentioned. Don't even wear a bowtie. Therefore, answer E is the correct answer.

2.   Keeping with the general impression that stereotypes concerning the insurance industry are valid, the only possible outfit you should wear to an interview at an insurance company would be the dullest thing in your closet. Although bowtie and suspenders might seem the right level of nerdiness, nerdy is not what insurance companies are looking for (at least not primarily), so answer C is wrong. Answer D, a cheap blue suit, would be the best answer. Answers A and E are a bit too trendy. Answer B, slippers, should stay in the house at all times.

3.   This question was not as difficult as you might have expected. Answer A is wrong because it presupposes that law firms don't maintain an atmosphere. While law firms might not have the most light-hearted

atmosphere and it might be like working in a pressure cooker, it actually does have a nitrogen-oxygen atmosphere at stand pressure of one atmosphere at sea level. Answer B is wrong because no one would mistake Santa Claus for an attorney, or vice versa. Answer D is wrong because you should never wear sweats anywhere. Answer E might be a bit too revealing. Therefore, answer C, the basic suit, would be the best choice for your law firm interview.

4. We really can't say why lawyers' clothes look different, so although you might have wanted answer B to be correct, only answer A is correct for sure.

Chapter 14 Take-Aways

Lots of lawyers like to dress to impress. Others like to dress in what is most comfortable. Some even like to look like an idiot or a dork. How would you dress if you worked in a law firm? Style is more important than you might have guessed.

1. Wear a suit (not sweatsuit or spacesuit or bathingsuit).

2. If you have a casual office, then you will have to develop your own style.

3. Develop a style that will make you appear impressive.

4. Don't develop a style that will make you appear like a dork.

Romance & the Law

If love is war, then what is litigation?

This chapter should probably be the subject of an entire book on relationships between highly stressed people, but frankly I can't be bothered with such nonsense.

Answering illegal questions

One particular experience stands out for me regarding marital bliss and the law. I was having an interview at some hole-in-the-wall slimly little law firm. The typically gruff fat-faced managing partner was interviewing me. One of the questions he asked me whether or not I was married. He's not supposed to ask me that question – there are laws against asking that. Nevertheless, I answered.

My answer to an illegal question: no, I was not married

but I was involved in a long distance romance.

The upshot was that when I said that I wasn't married he shook his head slightly in a disapproving way. Jeez, I'm not married; is this going to be a problem, I thought to myself.

Later, I found out that he was on his third wife. He must think that he is an expert at negotiation and conflict resolution.

Although I talked with him a while longer and then met another partner and actually got an offer, my mind had checked out of the interview. Next law firm, please.

Love and the Law

Whether in law school or in a firm, you or someone you know will develop a romance. When the law enters the picture, that lovely romance might appear a bit different.

The romance may be between two law students who provide an inspiration to the rest of the student body that love still exists.

It could be the illicit romance of two law firm colleagues having a torrid affair while working on some case that keeps them in the office past midnight every day. That romance might have a different effect than proving that love still exists. It also provides a lot of conversation filler amongst the law firm staff.

Office romance provides gossip topics.

But you might say *romance is beautiful.* After I stop

laughing, I would agree that romance is beautiful, but some of these relationships are far from romantic. And with the added third partner, *Stress*, romance can be quite difficult in the law.

Romance is more difficult
in a legal setting.

Romance is difficult in a legal setting simply because one or more of the participants is engaged in a highly stressful profession, has been trained in the art of nitpicking and the language of legalese, and is most likely an ambitious person who will put their career ahead of their interpersonal relationships.

That's the *obvious* slapping you in the face.

Let's take a look at various possible relationships and predict outcomes.

Pre-law student with anyone

For some reason, pre-law students feel like they are a bit special. By special, I don't mean in the *Special Olympics* sense or the *special education* sense but in the arrogant *I am better than you because I take pre-law* sense.

If someone was taking pre-engineering, or pre-French, or pre-history, it would all sound so weird that we would laugh. A collective hearty laugh, not just a guffaw or chuckle.

But, you say, there is pre-med as a major. And I'd say, yes, an even more arrogant bunch.

Nonetheless, we should all realize from the start that taking pre-*anything* means you haven't taken the thing yet.

Worse is that in pre-law, interesting constitutional law cases are usually discussed. These are exactly the type of cases that as an attorney you will never see.[67]

Real life and school and can be so divergent sometimes.[68]

Anyway, back to romance. We have to realize from the start that romance between unequal partners is bound to cause problems.

Here, the inequality is at best only wishful thinking on the part of the pre-law student. The not-pre-law student actually has a major and maybe even one that will put them on an actual career path. However, the pre-law student is still in the wanting stage. Not quite there yet, and won't even be quite there yet when they graduate. They will graduate with a degree in something that necessitates getting another degree. Now that's an accomplishment! Or so thinks that pre-law student.

Who would take a major that only leads to needing more schooling? First answer that pops into my head is someone who doesn't want to work.

So someone who is destined to make no money and rack up huge student loans will actually feel superior to someone getting a degree in a field that will get them a real job.

We'll avoid qualifying used-car salesman as a career

---

[67] That's after your *pre* years

[68] For *sometimes* read *always*.

move.

Come again? Yes, the *pre* student will feel superior. Then, if that's not odd enough, the non-*pre* student might feel that the *pre* student is somehow superior, too. That is life. Unless both worship the *pre* student, the relationship is bound for turmoil.

If the non-*pre* student wakes up and gets out before they actually have to deal with a law student and the law student's loans, then perhaps there's justice in the world.

What?! You wanted in depth relationship advice here?! Don't date a pre-law student. Or, date them but don't marry them. Marry the lawyer if the student loan debt is individual property and not community property. It will make for fewer headaches during the divorce.

As for the pre-law student: go out with anyone not pre-law because they will get a job and support you while you ply your own selfish motives and study for another three years.

How was that for relationship advice?

Two law students

It happens. People get horny and tend to mate within the same distance that rats mate. This is Discovery Channel stuff, so it's gotta be true.

Now, on a rare occasion, perhaps they were both pre-law and got into this same law school. Yeah, perhaps not. That is such a rarity that it's not even a standard Hollywood plot. Go figure!

Were talking here about two people, students, who are both taking torts or contracts. They meet for a study session and one thing leads to another.

Studying together
can lead to sex.

Perhaps one is a third-year student and the other and incoming first year.[69]

The third year student — their power and prestige — impresses the first year. Perhaps so much so that at the beach party they meet and go off and have wild sex on the beach for hours. The rest of the party has left and they have to hitch a ride back to their dorms.

Unfortunately one or both of them is already in our relationship with which means sad feelings will soon ensue.

Maintain one
intimate relationship
at a time.

However if they are both free, the sad feelings will take longer to ensue because they will have the chance to get to know each other and find out after two years that they had nothing in common except torts, contracts, and a need for sex.

---

[69] Regarding *incoming students*, please make no innuendo here, at least not more than intended.

Try to have something in common besides the law.

Sure they may also find out that they like same authors, such as the famous authors listed below:

Geoffrey Chaucer[70]

Anthony Trollope[71]

Charles Dickens[72]

However, it's unlikely that anyone would ever like all three. So, two law students may hook-up. In the parlance of dating at school, *hooking up* implies a devoted or committed relationship that could last longer than 1 semester but, in actuality, probably not more than 3 weeks, and usually only 1 night.

Take it to the next level.

But what if these two lovebirds should decide to take their relationship to the next level: the *splitting the rent* level.

---

[70] Geoffrey Chaucer is remembered as the author of *Canterbury Tales*, one of the greatest epic works of literature.

[71] Anthony Trollope was a leading English novelist of the middle 19th Century. He published 47 novels and 16 books in several other genres. Some of his stuff has even been on Public Television.

[72] Reading Dickens makes me ill. Even the thought of plodding through one of his tomes is enough to make me…, excuse me; perhaps you like reading Dickens droning on and on. What about Madame DeFarge?

Yes, they love to study all the time, they have all the same friends, and they split the rent.[73]

Oh, yes, and sex might be involved. Sex might lead to the management of stress, or so it is thought. But most likely it's the reverse.

So, two law students living together: doomed.

You want a more comprehensive analysis?

Select the reason it is doomed: stress; lack of interest in each other as a person; an apartment comes available that one can afford without a roommate; a *roommate with benefits* when the benefits cease is just a constant annoyance; or, they wake up from their dream world to a nightmare.

We had one couple at my law school who didn't breakup upon graduation. They might still be together. Many would say that they were really nice people who were in love. I would even say it. On the other hand, perhaps they were suffering some mental illness. We will never know.[74]

Law student and non-law person meeting before law school

Doomed. Hopeless. Move on and get over it.

---

[73] For *friends* read *fellow students* because at law school you really don't have any friends. Also, in English we tend to call simple acquaintances *friends*.

[74] Actually, I could easily find out if they're still together, but I don't think I'd have the stomach for that.

Face it; law school is three years of hell. A person goes through more stress and change in the first semester of first year than most people do in a lifetime.

No, I'm not exaggerating here. You might think I'm exaggerating, but I'm not exaggerating.

For the most part, the other person (the non-law person) has no clue, can't relate, and has a hard time understanding the stress, etc. All jokes aside, it is the rare relationship that started before law school that lasts thereafter. If you think yours will be the exception, then it's back to the bookstore for you for you to get real relationship advice books. Not to say that the book you are currently reading, i.e. this book, isn't a real relationship advice book, but since you found it classified under humor (or law, if they didn't look at it close enough when they filed it) — blah, blah, whatever.

Law student meeting non-law person while law student is in law school

Now for the relationship that has a chance. Why? Because the law student has passed through the first year. Second year is nothing and third year is a joke, so meeting someone at this point has the highest likelihood of success. See, I can be positive. Of course how long it will last is another matter entirely. What? That's not positive enough?

A lawyer and another lawyer

In exploring the convivial relationships that occur

between lawyers, the reader is advised that the party of the first part and the party of the second part have no clue what trouble lies ahead of them.[75]

The main problem with lawyer/lawyer relationships is the fact that two high powered and driven people pack in an awful lot of nitpicking.

Is there any advantage? Surprisingly, yes.

Don't get all excited because I've being upbeat.

A major problem of a lawyer in relationship with a non-lawyer is that the non-lawyer may have a very difficult time in managing the types and amounts of stress that the lawyer faces from day to day. This lack of understanding can lead to added frustration on the part of both parties.[76]

The advantage, therefore, that the lawyer/lawyer relationship has is that usually both parties are aware of the negative aspects of the practice of law and are thusly prepared to deal with them.

This doesn't necessarily mean that the arguments decrease, but the types of arguments will be different. Arguments made maybe devoid of the typical *why must you come home so late* or *what do you mean that you can't do X today because you're so stressed*, or *I don't care what you say, nothing is more important than Aunt Edna's 70th*

---

[75] Oh, I forgot that I said in some earlier chapter that we wouldn't have any of the *party of the first part* crap. Sorry. I held out as long as I could.

[76] The *party of the first part and the party of the second part* — opps, sorry I wrote that again, just habit.

birthday party and you forgot to get the guacamole — how hard was that to get![77]

By the way, just to note the point, Aunt Edna doesn't particularly like guacamole (she doesn't even know what it is), so getting it wasn't really for her benefit. Arguments over Aunt Edna or guacamole can get particularly ugly.

Conclusion: lawyer/lawyer relationships may actually succeed. Just don't bet heavily on it.

A lawyer and a staff person

In the same sense that arguments needn't take on a lawyer/non-lawyer adversarial dimension, lawyer/paralegal or lawyer/legal secretary relationships might prove even better. Why? Because both relationship participants are aware of legal stress but one of them isn't a stress case.

Imagine this scenario: the lawyer comes home complaining about the Douglas case and how Gerald, the senior partner, is an ass. The paralegal or legal secretary can just reply *that's tragic dear*, and move on.

There is scientific evidence that this paralegal/legal secretary exception to the lawyer/non-lawyer relationship role might apply to other professions but we can't have a lengthy discussion of that here, now, can we?

One aspect that can prevent the lawyer/staff relationship from ever getting off the ground is the class structure

---

[77] Where X, the unknown, is actually known to one of the parties but might still be unknown to the other.

inherent in law firms.

There is a serf/noble analog concerning the relationships between partners and associates but there's an even more distinct divide between the attorneys and the staff. Yes, yes, and there's all that *who's got the power* stuff I discussed with the pre-law student. I didn't forget; I just didn't want to have to reiterate it.

You'll recall my Christmas party with the secretary who told me that I should get in the line for hors d'oeuvres and mingle with the partners.

Another example was as a friend of mine who was suddenly single after a long relationship. He began dating some of the female attorneys at the large Los Angeles law firm he worked at. He found the attorneys quite boring, though, because all they wanted to do was talk about the law and they had no outside interests.

I told him about the aforementioned secretary. She hadn't gathered all those exciting law school expenses but instead gathered real life experiences like working as a costume person for the movie industry or keeping a good-sized garden.

Naturally, costume design or knowing what vegetables are in season might only provide a limited set of conversations. However my point is that she was interesting in ways outside the law and my friend should look beyond lawyers to date. The class divisions were too much for him. He was unconvinced.

Eventually, though, he did marry the office manager at law firm he worked at some years later. Which proves me right, so there!

Associate lawyer and law firm partner

The lawyer/lawyer relationship can reach its breaking point when an associate and partner hit the romance circuit. The power difference is so great that this relationship is usually only an affair.

The older partner gets some young thing and the younger associate — not sure what the younger associate is thinking. Job advancement? A future well-earning spouse? Whenever the reward is, it might not be worth the karmic sacrifice.

We had a young female associate at the mythical law firm where Hamburger and Hotdog (from Chapter 13) were employed. She was "the other woman", having broken up the marriage of a partner at another firm and his wife. She never looked happy even though she was always getting flowers from that partner.

Her relationship provided the secretaries with lots of gossip topics such as why all the flowers, why did she have bruises all the time, and why was she always so sad looking.

Bad vibes all around.

Two thumbs down.

Two lawyers at different law firms

This whole analysis of relationships is well beyond the reasonable stage. Figure that lawyers from different law firms might actually meet, have a relationship, and something else. *Something else* simply means *something else* because, frankly, by this point it's all irrelevant.

Law firm partners

Partners aren't buying this book, so this section has been excised because it's extraneous.

Quiz concerning romance & the law

Romance and the law can be a dangerous mix. Answer the following questions after careful reflection.

1. Which relationship will survive the longest?
   a. Bob and Alice.
   b. Todd and Cynthia.
   c. Matthew and Penelope.
   d. Eric and Tanya.
   e. Dave and Elizabeth.

2. Why are people attracted to pre-law students?
   a. They want to be with someone who will incur a lot more student loan debt.
   b. Engineering students don't have a lot of TV shows exploring the glamour of engineering.
   c. As with buying a pre-owned car, the other person is thinking that they are getting some kind of bargain.
   d. They want to be crushed and humiliated later.
   e. Science is still wondering, too.

3. True or False: Romance is possible even in the legal profession.
   a. True.
   b. False.
   c. Neither.

Quiz Answers

Do you believe in romance? Do you believe in love? Do you respect the law? Who cares? We're all doomed to have relationships. It's best just to sit back and watch other people's relationships explode.

1. B is the correct answer because Todd and Cynthia are both vacuous in the brain area. The other relationships are doomed for a number of reasons that probably have to do with their being associated with the practice of law. Tragic.

2. All the answers are possible, but the most correct answer is E. Who knows why people are attracted to pre-law students. There is no good reason. Sorry.

3. The correct answer is A, True, or else I wouldn't have written this chapter. You should realize, however, that the quality of the romance is what really matters. On the bright side, there is someone out there for everyone (a lesson we learned from the Steve Martin movie *L.A. Story*).

Chapter 15 Take-Aways

Romance and the law can be a tricky subject. In this past chapter we explored the possible variations of how someone involved in the law can get together with someone else. I know it was exhaustive in its completeness, so below we have only the most salient points.

1. Romance involving a lawyer or law student will be problematic at best.

2. Love is wonderful.

3. Try to overlook the nitpicking and focus on the arguing.

4. Don't think of Judge Learned Hand when having sex.

CONCLUSION

Stress:

Your new soulmate

Quacks on television promise to find you your soulmate after you fill out a questionnaire. You can then be linked with another idiot who fell for the same scam. As a lawyer, you have no need to take any tests except the bar. Because once you take that test and pass, your future companionship is assured.

Your answers on the bar exam will link you with your soulmate. If you pass, your mate for the rest of your working life will be **Stress**.

Not just any run-of-the-mill stress, but the stress that comes from constantly being in a win or lose situation. There are win-win situations, but you'll never have to worry about them. Nope. The sweet smelling threat of losing is always in the air and *Stress* is bringing the pungent bouquet.

When Stress Calls on You

I recall the stress of taking my first deposition. It was a wrongful death case where a family was suing our client for having manufactured its crane so poorly that the father/husband fell to his death. We eventually won the case, but early on, you couldn't tell how the case would end.

They were suing our poor innocent crane manufacturer, so they had some monetary interest in the case. I had to take the deposition of the teenage daughter and ask her questions like how often did she spend time with her dad — you know, quality time. How much money they could get would depend in part in what kind of father/daughter relationship existed. Fun, fun, fun. Not the type of questions a nice person wants to ask someone after her father has died.

My co-counsel representing another company was so nervous asking his follow-up questions that after I got through with mine, he got the teenage girl so anxious that she ran out of the room several times crying.

I was more fortunate because I had my own private crisis prior to the deposition while I was outlining my questions. I wrote a letter to myself asking myself how could I have taken up such a career that would put me in such a situation. How would I have liked it had someone been asking me questions if my dad had died?

Empathy is a serious calculation all lawyers should be aware of.[78]

---

[78] Attention: preachiness, but still a good idea.

My part of the deposition went without incident and luckily for me future depositions never proved as emotionally difficult.

Nonetheless, *Stress* has been my constant companion throughout my practice.

When You Call on Stress

Years later, in a totally fictitious situation, I was defending an expert in a deposition. I don't recall much about the case but I remember how confident I had become in taking depositions. *Stress* was finally defeated, or so I thought.

Just to review: there is no attorney-client privilege with an expert. And, don't forget that the term *expert* is so loosely construed that your Uncle Ernie who spits pistachio nut shells farther than anyone you know would be considered an expert, especially if he says what you want him to say and you pay him $1000 for a day of his testimony.

I was opposed in this deposition by some *bowtie and suspenders* wearing attorney with perfectly coifed hair. He also had the courtesy to bring along a young female associate who attended the *Beauty School of Law*. She did nothing except provide a distraction to my expert and me.[79]

This kind of associate we condescendingly refer to as a *show-blonde associate*.[80]

---

[79] Probably not my expert because he seemed to be neuter.

[80] I'm sure there are female brunette versions and male versions

The opposing counsel, her boss, was also so power-crazed that her sexuality was a non-issue.[81]

As the deposition proceeded, I made it a point to object to preserve my objections for trial, which was allowed in the old days. When I first objected, I saw that the opposing counsel got upset. There was no reason to get upset because except for rare circumstances, the witness would answer the question even if there was an objection. Nonetheless, he got upset. He got more upset as I objected again. Perhaps *Stress* could be my friend?

I objected again and again, more calm with each objection as my opponent got more and more upset. His face turned redder and redder. I thought that with his bowtie so tight his head would pop off, but I wasn't that lucky.

Finally, I objected to a question as outside the scope of my expert's knowledge. The opposing attorney slammed his hand down on the table, and pointed at me with the other, demanding that I stipulate to that fact.

He wanted me to stipulate (entered as a point of fact in the case) that the expert didn't know what he was talking about. Yeah, like I was going to do that! Again, I said that I was merely preserving my objections for trial. Opposing counsel's head was ready to explode. What fun!

But my fun was to end. As opposing counsel questioned my expert, my poor dopey expert answered a question totally opposite to what I wanted or expected. Nevertheless, I

---

but I don't know them off-hand.

[81] For attorneys like him, power is their sex-substitute.

maintained my blank lawyer look on my face. I asked if we could stop the deposition for a moment so I could have word with my expert. As I mentioned before, being that there is no attorney-client privilege with the expert, the opposing counsel can ask him to repeat anything I say to him.

I decided to make *Stress* my friend again, as if I wasn't doing that enough by torturing the opposing counsel.

Leaving the conference room where we were conducting the deposition, I took the expert aside and asked him if he was feeling okay, to which he said yes. I told him to make sure he listens to each question before answering. Then, in this totally fictitious scenario, I told him the clincher: I said that opposing counsel was an ass.

My strategy, since he would naturally be asked to recite our conversation, was that I would be able to insult the opposing counsel without having to say it myself. That's a renegade attorney's strategy for having opposing counsel's head explode (Attention nerds: don't tie those ties so tight).

Sure enough, we returned to the conference room and opposing counsel, thinking he had put one over on me asked the expert, "so I supposed that your attorney was quite dissatisfied with your answer to my last question?"

His grin was quickly wiped off his face when my expert answered *no*. The expert gave the attorney a blank look like he had no clue what he was talking about.

Stage one: red face engaged.

"Well, as you know," opposing counsel, who was getting even redder in the face, told the expert, "I have the right to learn everything that was said between you and your attorney."

The expert nodded.

Opposing counsel asked, "So what did learned counsel say to you when he took you from the room?"

He must have thought I was an idiot, yet now I'm *learned counsel*. Too bad for him.

The expert said, "He asked how I was feeling."

"Is that all?" the opposing counsel asked, exasperatedly.

"He also told me to listen to the questions before I answered."

The beauty of it (no, not the blond female attorney) was the sight of that arrogant, perfectly coifed head about to explode and create a mess.

Stage two reached.

"Is that all he said?!" the attorney shouted.

Internally, I'm chanting to myself, "tell him, tell him, tell him."

But to my chagrin, the expert said, "no that was all."

Damn. No stage 3.

On the other hand, an exploding head creates a tremendous mess. Besides getting the show-associate all disgusting, I would have had to dry-clean my suit a week earlier than I planned.

So, take it from a renegade: *Stress*, although a constant companion, is unlikely to become your friend.

When Stress Gives You a Break

It can be fun to run into a courthouse where a paralegal

from your firm is already waiting for you (like on those television police dramas where the supporting cast is already on the scene before the star detective shows up). The paralegal hands you the case files in huge red file folders. You ask a few questions like *what is the hearing about* or *whom do we represent.* Usually these questions will go unanswered and you'll actually have to read the file.

You can read the file while you wait to be called by the clerk of the court. If you're on defense, at least you can hear the plaintiff's counsel ramble on so you can get some clue about what the controversy is about. If you happen to be the plaintiff's counsel, you'll have to learn to read faster lest you become really pathetic (in the eyes of the court).

When I first started out practicing law, naturally I was a bit more prepared. But, nothing can prepare you for nature.

My first court appearance in a California court and I was bit nervous. My companion *Stress*, was second-chairing me on the case. More pointedly, I needed that chair in the room down the hall — the one that has a hole in it and water swirling in it.[82]

I was second in line to be called into the court and as I stood waiting while the first case's attorneys were called up to the judge for their hearing. I raised my hand. The judge, a friendly looking middle-aged black woman, acknowledged me.

"Your honor, do I have time to run to the bathroom?"

The judge smiled and said, "go for it" while

---

[82] The toilet.

simultaneously making a *clenched fist yanking down a subway strap* movement.

Kewl judge.

And she was right. I made it back in time and won my first court hearing.

Obviously, clearing one's bowels or bladder before a hearing is the way to go. It adds pre-hearing clarity. It also keeps our companion, *Stress*, out of the courtroom.

When Stress Tricks You

Don't forget that as your companion, *Stress* is there all the time for you, even when you least expect it. Certainly, *Stress* will accompany you to court. But sometimes, *Stress* is sent by your own firm's partnership to keep you honest.

About 3 or 4 years into my career, I still had never lost a motion in court. Not only did this make me popular, but it also made me popularly hated. No one likes the smug idiot who hasn't been humbled.

In their collective wisdom, my firm sent me to a hearing before a judge they later told me was called the *hanging judge* of that court.

My firm had missed a hearing because no one attended it. As it turned out two attorneys who could have appeared were not notified because our new computer system had cancelled them, each thinking the other was on the case. I was sent to a hearing to avoid our firm being sanctioned by the court for non-attendance.

When I got to court, it turned out to be punishment day.

Several attorneys standing in a row in front of the court — the judge fining each attorney as their case came up.

I was last (story of my life). The judge barked at me demanding to know why no one showed up at the prior hearing. I explained the computer glitch and apologized.

The judge said he was going to sanction us several thousand dollars but he liked my explanation so he only fined me $250. For me, $250 was quite a loss.

I thought, in all modesty that I could get off without a fine.[83]

When I returned to my firm, I was asked how it went.

"We were fined $250," I said.

Before I could add that I was sorry, I had a partner slapping me on the back and thanking me.

I didn't understand.

He explained that there was a mandatory fine and the $250 was the least the judge could fine us. I was a hero. I still felt like I lost, though, but my egomania soon returned.

Stress had accompanied me to court and I needn't have worried. Silly me. And that is only motion practice.

When Stress Follows You

Going to trial is even worse. When the trial is a big one, *Stress* not only is your companion but brings along other *Stress* companions that have some free time. In other words, the stress levels become quite high.

---

[83] That's not modesty; that's egomania.

One friend, the attorney I would go to if I had a problem, because they don't come more kick-ass than her, had a job where she had 20 cases at once and was arguing each of them as they went to trial.

She worked for a firm where their client, a large insurance company, never liked to settle a case. So she was constantly at trial. If she hadn't later gotten married to a very pleasant guy, I'm sure *Stress* was hoping to carry her away.

When You Make Stress Your Primary Companion

Stress also becomes a companion when we invite it along. An old friend of mine recently told me how boring I was when I was working for one of the biggest firms in New York City. She would call me up to go to a party — I had to work. She would call me up to do dinner — I had to work. Boring — because I was working all the time.

I had no time for a girlfriend when I could enjoy the constant company of *Stress*. And I find that many people decide to even forego their spouses to enjoy extended time with *Stress*.

Once, I met a pretty female attorney at a health-supplements store just south of Grand Central Station. It was a place I frequented, not to meet women, but to get the one miracle supplement that would promote wellness and defeat stress. Not finding it on the shelves and seeing this harried woman in search of the same miraculous wonder, we began talking.

Seemed like she knew *Stress* as well as I did.

As you will come to know, *Stress* has a lot of interesting stories. Talking about *Stress* seemed to bond us, at least momentarily, in some new kind of reality. Anyway, she gave me her card and I said I would call her to get together for dinner or something.[84]

A week so later, I was sitting at my desk at 11 o'clock at night. Unfortunately, 11:00 p.m. is not an abnormal time for lawyers to be working. I saw the card that this woman had given me and thought *gee, perhaps if I actually call her I might get a life.*

Yes, life is a bit constricted when working at 11 p.m. after having arrived at work at 8 a.m. Thoughts get even more muddled when quitting time looks like the ever more distant 3 a.m. the next morning.

I figure no way will this woman be at her office, another huge law firm across the street on Park Avenue from mine. So I called to leave a message and to try to be more exacting in defining *or something* as, say, lunch. When I called, the phone hardly rang once when she answered. She was at work, too. If I looked out of my window facing Park Avenue, perhaps I could see her?

I asked her to lunch sometime next week, but she was too busy. She sounded quite frustrated. She was preparing for trial. Ah, *Stress* was in the room with her, and *Stress* hates infidelity. There would be no launch date. *Stress* had booked her calendar solid.

While dating for a single attorney can be hellish — so

---

[84] *Or something*: a vagary not solely employed by lawyers.

too can be the married life of the attorney. Divorce or just very unhappy marriages seem to be a result of practicing law because spouses often seem to not want to share their mate with *Stress*.

My favorite example of über-stress is the two-attorney marriage. It's almost polygamous because each attorney brings along their own *Stress*. Perhaps sometimes they switch off so that the two extra *Stress*es spend time together and the spouses can enjoy each other's company alone. I doubt it, though, because *Stress* probably doesn't have a spare room.

Your New Soulmate is Stress

All in all, *Stress* will be your constant companion from the time you start practicing law until the time you die. How *Stress* handles you or, really, how you handle *Stress*, is critical to your survival as an attorney. And while you may survive, it would be even better to thrive and enjoy being a lawyer.

Perhaps the best advice to give would be to understand that no job is perfect, no job can meet the hype from TV and the movies, no job that gives such power and money can be obtained without many hurdles to cross, and no job can be so dire that we can't laugh about it once in a while.

I hope that this book has at least put a smile or two on your face. More smiles might need to be generated by you yourself. Just don't be seen smiling when grumpy senior partners walk by your office.

Quiz concerning stress

Stress can be you constant companion. But, as with any companion, the relationship can depend more on your perceptions and expectations than on reality. Then again, what is reality?

1. Based on the reading, what would be the best caption for the badly drawn picture below?

    a.   Man overwhelmed by *Stress*.
    b.   Man coping with *Stress*.
    c.   Man using *Stress* to his advantage.
    d.   Man helping *Stress*.
    e.   Man devoid of *Stress*.

2. Complete the following sentence. If you become a lawyer, you would have to deal with a lot of _____
    a.   onions.
    b.   horses, ponies, zebras, and statues with

saddles.

 c. movie analogies.

 d. zombies.

 e. stress.

3. Can you make *Stress* your friend?

 a. *Stress* is not really a person, so you cannot make *Stress* your friend because it just doesn't make sense to make it your friend.

 b. *Stress* is a feeling of anxiety caused by feeling out of control, so you cannot make *Stress* your friend because it is a reaction or an emotion and it just doesn't make sense to make it your friend.

 c. *Stress* is an evil entity, akin to the Devil, so you cannot make Stress your friend.

 d. It says in the conclusion that *Stress* can be made your friend, but it's a lie, so you cannot make *Stress* your friend.

 e. It says in the conclusion that *Stress* can be made your friend, so of course it is possible, even if difficult.

Quiz Answers

Certainly I went a little deep with this end chapter, with all those stories about *Stress*. And how about personifying *Stress*, that was inventive, wasn't it. Okay, maybe not that deep, maybe not that inventive. What is funny about the practice of law? Very little. Although it need not be so dire. Did you see how *Stress* played a part of each question in this chapter? That is because the chapter was about *Stress*.

1. The picture, although badly drawn by the author, supposedly illustrates a man being overwhelmed by *Stress*. Although the drawing is bad and could possibly refer to almost anything, you still could only pick Answer A because the conclusion was about *Stress* and none of the other answers made any sense.

2. The Answer is A. If you become a lawyer, you would have to deal with a lot of stress. Answers B and D, horse and zombies, are possibilities, but stress is far more likely. Movie analogies, answer C, only applies in small Los Angeles enclaves like Century City. Answer A, onions, only applies to victims of the Food Channel.

3. Answers A and B are very close yet only one of them can be right, so they are both wrong. Answer C would make sense unless you read the conclusion,

because the conclusion does discuss making *Stress* your friend. However, since this book is a silly book, you cannot expect answer E to be the correct answer. Answer D is the best answer, because it must be a lie that you can make *Stress* your friend. Maybe not. Maybe it's better if we make E the correct response

Conclusion Take-Aways

Stress is a part of life. If you are a lawyer or a law student, the stress could get so bad that you might think you are chained to a nagging spouse. After a while, you will wish that you had a nagging spouse instead of all the legal stress.

1. Lawyers not only create stress in others but also carry it around as unchecked baggage wherever they go.

2. Practicing law creates stress and it doesn't get any better with more practice, it just gets old.

3. Law, law, law. Stress, stress, stress.

4. Smile; it can only get worse.

About the Author

When not writing supposedly humorous books about the legal profession, Eric Zyla does serious work on technology litigation, the strategic use of intellectual property, and related business transactions.

Eric is a lawyer with an MBA and prior experience as an electrical engineer. He is admitted to the bar in New York and California and is a registered attorney with the US Patent & Trademark Office. He is the author of several other (quite serious) books on the law and international business risk analysis.

About the Book

The Renegade Lawyer satirizes today's legal profession, tackling such topics as how majoring in political science is pointless, how the way the law is taught (the Socratic method) would have Socrates turning over in his grave, how to lose friends by constantly arguing and nitpicking (important legal skills), how court decisions result from what the judge had for breakfast, and how stress becomes a lawyer's constant companion.

The book offers advice based on actual experiences, such as don't wear short pants to a luncheon with your law school dean or slippers in your law firm partner's office.

You will learn how to write rejection letters to law firms before they reject you and discover what movies to watch to overcome law school burnout.

This humorous send-up of the law is intended for anyone who enjoys seeing the legal profession lampooned. It starts by asking whether a lawyer can smile. Hopefully, you will be smiling after reading it. However, if you are a lawyer, make sure that you smile with your office door close